Shortcut

GETTING THROUGH TO PEOPLE
WHO SLOW YOU DOWN

BRIAN TOLLE

authorHOUSE®

AuthorHouse™
1663 Liberty Drive
Bloomington, IN 47403
www.authorhouse.com
Phone: 1-800-839-8640

First published by AuthorHouse   06/18/2011

ISBN: 978-1-4634-2523-4 (sc)
ISBN: 978-1-4634-2522-7 (ebk)

Library of Congress Control Number: 2011910129

Printed in the United States of America

To my father who inspired me.

Contents

Introduction

The fact that you are reading this suggests you are struggling with a degree of frustration in getting certain people to move faster to do what you need them to do. You've probably had the same conversation, on the same issue, with the same person, more than once and have thought, "what is going on here, why can't I get through to this person?" What started out as disappointment in someone's work has now grown into full-blown frustration. When these employees don't "get it," you find yourself spending more time explaining things and less time getting the job done and moving on to the next task. You think to yourself,

> *I can do it faster and better myself. So why waste time and energy trying to explain to certain direct reports what they need to do and how to do it? I'll just do it myself.*

As tempting as this can be, doing both your job and their job is not a long-term strategy. What makes this situation so critical is that you manage people and work in teams. Your superiors expect you to get things done through others. The longer you are in management, the more others evaluate you on your ability to get things done through your employees and peers. Otherwise, your company is paying for a pricey individual contributor and not a manager. Your department's productivity begins to lag as you take on more and more responsibility that should belong to your employees. Eventually all of this catches up with you and you find your career ladder noticeably shortened.

You could also be in a situation in which the company you lead is in desperate need of change and adaptation. You need to influence an entire organization, its very culture. You might assume that the grimmer the circumstances facing the organization, the greater the likelihood the culture will be motivated to adapt to survive and move forward. No matter the circumstance, the pace of organizational change is often that of a snail.

Now back to your frustration. *Why can't I get through to this person (or organization), no matter what I say or do?* The fact is you'll never get through if you're not speaking their "language."

Case in Point

I was recently in a brainstorming session with market research and R&D managers at a Fortune 50 client. The marketing manager turns to the R&D technical lead and asks, "can you give me a list of all possible technologies out there?" She was speaking the language of high level summary of the universe of possibilities. The technical lead, on the other hand, translated it as "give me information on the technologies we are capable of delivering in the near future." Simple miscommunication? Little business impact? Not if you're trying to stretch the innovation possibilities and the R&D lead disqualifies longer term technologies because they're not ready now. That's one reason why innovation at some companies looks like the same old stuff re-packaged.

This book is fundamentally about understanding, recognizing, and speaking the language of different ways of approaching work – what some call behavioral styles. You yourself have a preferred way of operating and a big focus of your style is getting things done, working through obstacles to move things along. Everything around the value you place on progress constitutes the language of your behavioral style. Most likely you've been thwarted to date with some individuals simply because you are not speaking their language. You've assumed everyone speaks your language. That's not how the world works.

This book is your guide to learning the language of different behavioral styles. Becoming adept at speaking the "style language" of every person and culture you need to influence will open your eyes to more effective ways of motivating people. What's in it for you is lower frustration and greater influence. But only if you approach the situation like a traveler in a foreign land – you can't expect to get through to people if you don't speak their language. What's more, relying on others to make the switch to your language has its own set of risks. Given your frustration, it sounds like it is time for a visit to the language lab of behavioral styles.

Format of Book

Your time is valuable. You have challenging situations with certain individuals that are distracting you from moving things forward. This book is designed to give you digestible amounts of information that you can act upon sooner rather than later. Helping you score early small successes will help you stay motivated to learn more. You'll see a quicker return on your investment of time and money the sooner you start trying out new techniques and strategies instead of reading the entire book cover-to-cover.

Part One (page 11) gives you a quick, first round list of actions you can experiment with to get you trying out new tactics with the person you have in mind.

Part Two (page 19) goes deeper into why this person says and does the things they do. You'll learn about the four behavioral styles, how to recognize the style preferences of people you interact with, what motivates them, and how to speak their particular "dialect." You'll also hear each style explained in the words of people with that particular style preference.

Part Three (page 81) describes common combination of styles in a person. We all use some combination of two of the four behavioral styles. You'll learn how these combinations play out in a person's behavior and the inherent tensions the style combinations pose for the individual.

The Practice (page 85) contains a group exercise to help people practice how to speak the dialects of behavioral styles most opposite to their own preferred style. This workshop is great for both teambuilding and improving cross-functional communication and collaboration.

PART ONE

Step 1: Focus

To get the most out of this effort, it is best to start with one individual who will serve as your laboratory. Experimenting in a less risky situation will put you in a stronger position to apply your insights and new skills to more demanding circumstances. Don't pick a direct report, peer, or superior who is your greatest challenge. Rather, focus on a relationship that has room for improvement and one you feel you have a good chance of improving with the right insights and strategies. The best choice is one in which you feel you could make some mistakes with low risk of consequences.

Write his or her name (or an alias to maintain confidentiality) below to help you maintain your focus as you read this guide.

Name: _____   Name: _____

Step 2: Name Your Frustration

With this person in mind, pick one of the four descriptions below that captures what you find frustrating about working with him or her. These descriptions are not meant to be all-inclusive but merely a starting point to get you headed in the right direction.

Profile #1

He/she is a bit too independent at times. This can result in duplicate efforts and time wasted in "re-inventing the wheel" activities. The desire to finish projects as quickly as possible drives him/her at times to compromise quality and coordination with key stakeholders. Often you need to step in and repair the damage they have done to a project or departmental relationship. (see page 14)

Profile #2

He/she seems to spend more time cheerleading an effort rather than getting the work done. He/she seems to enjoy being in social situations and interacting with lots of people. As a result, he/she is not always on top of everything to get the job done as quickly as it should. He/she ends up spending too much time talking about the task rather than doing the task. (see page 15)

Profile #3

He/she is often resistant to new ideas or ways of doing things. He/she asks a lot of questions about the change, such as why, why now, who will be affected, what will happen when, who will do what, etc. He/she can't seem to take the first step without having a complete plan in hand. He/she is more likely to drag their feet than openly challenge the change. (see page 16)

Profile #4

He/she is a perfectionist to his/her own detriment. He/she often slows down progress by checking and re-checking work or analyzing the situation from every conceivable angle. He/she comes across as a procrastinator because he/she can't sign off on data or action until he/she has completed a thorough evaluation. He/she is often critical of decisions others make with incomplete data or analysis. (see page 17)

Step 3: Quick Strategies

General guidelines for using the following strategies:

• The text in italics is a suggested script that you can experiment with when talking with this person.

• The remaining text provides you with insights for you to consider and test out with the individual.

• As you try out these suggestions, be prepared to observe closely how the person reacts, both verbally and through body language. (Managing remotely will require you to be extra diligent in listening for verbal cues as well as taking full advantage of face-to-face opportunities when they are available.) What seems to resonate with him/her and what doesn't? The chances of an instant change of behavior are slim but take comfort in an incremental softening of their behavor. These can be indications that you are speaking their "dialect" and they are responding positively to your new ability.

Profile #1

Getting their attention:

Understand that I want you to move things quickly as much as you do. So you need to do certain things so none of us wastes time circling back and fixing things. That's why I need you to use these (methods, processes, people) the first time so you don't end up creating obstacles for yourself further down the road.

Music to their ears:

- *I know you're busy so I'll get right to the point.*
- *Here's the bottom line...*
- *This is an opportunity for you to advance.*
- *Here are the actions we're/I'm taking...*
- *The project has hit some roadblocks but here's what we're doing to get it back on track.*

Sprinkle these words here and there:

progress, proceed, move forward, leap ahead, push ahead, gain ground, drive, results, output, yield, decisions made, actions taken

Hint:

Start with the end of the story, first. Or, give them the headline version of what you need to tell them, first. Don't be afraid to be direct with him/her. If professionally done and in a constructive manner, he/she will be more open to the message and will likely respect you for your candidness.

Profile #2

Getting their attention:

I really appreciate all the enthusiasm you have brought to this project. Everyone involved seems pumped up. I'm concerned though that the team isn't fully aware of the timeframe for delivering. The more it feels vague, the greater the likelihood people will start to get de-motivated. If that happens the project will suffer and it will reflect poorly on you and the team.

Music to their ears...

- *This is how we can generate some excitement around the project...*
- *Do anything fun this weekend?*
- *We're here today to recognize you for all your contributions to this company...*
- *We've got some ideas we want your input on...*
- *Here's the impact your ideas and hard work had on our customers...*

Sprinkle these words here and there:

fantastic, awesome, fabulous, extraordinary, exceptional, remarkable, phenomenal, dynamic, exciting, positive, energy, we

Hint:

Allow for a certain amount of social conversation to build a foundation of rapport and keep a positive tone in your words and body language.

Profile #3

Getting their attention:

Thanks for taking the time to meet with me. As we start this new initiative, I wanted to get your perspective and insights. I'm interested in hearing what we can do to make sure the transition to the new way goes smoothly with minimal impact to everyone involved. I know how much you care about this (team, department, company) so I want to make sure I incorporate your ideas where I can.

Music to their ears:

- *Let me know when you would like to check in with me as you get into this new project.*
- *We've/I've thought about how this could impact the team members and here's a plan to make things go smoothly...*
- *I appreciate what you did to make the team successful.*
- *So it sounds like we agree on these next steps...*
- *Here are the resources available to you if you need them to get this project done...*

Sprinkle these words here and there:

consistent, reliable, stable, steady, establish, dependable, sound, trusting, anticipate, think it through, plan, process

Hint:

Ensure a two-way conversation, avoiding interrupting them when they're talking, inviting them to share their concerns and ideas in a safe atmosphere, and asking clarifying questions to fully understand their points-of-view.

Profile #4

Getting their attention:

I want us to execute this project flawlessly. Your standards and attention to details are going to play a big part in accomplishing this. The risk though is that the time it will take us to hit a level of perfection will put us at a significant disadvantage in the marketplace. I need your help in striking the right balance so we don't compromise quality for the sake of speed.

Music to their ears:

- *You received the documents I sent you so I would like to find out what questions you have.*
- *I'll create a spreadsheet so we can analyze the data.*
- *Based on my analysis, this would be the optimal way to proceed.*
- *This approach would adhere to our standards for quality...*
- *Your attention to detail paid off with a quality output.*

Sprinkle these words here and there:

standards, systematic approach, methodology, standard operating procedures (SOP's), deliberate, efficient, thorough, well prepared, reasoning, rationale, analyze, assess

Hint:

Start at the beginning of the story and be prepared with data to back up what you are saying. Use insights from the data to prepare a robust and thorough process you can share ahead of time. Acknowledge strong processes deliver strong results.

PART TWO

Meaning Behind the Behavior

The four profiles we have explored so far are actually four distinct behavioral styles that researchers have identified over the years. This chapter gives you:

- an overview of the categories of human behavior that form these four styles,
- the particular preferences of each style that form the basis of their "dialect" and
- how best to use this information to get through to an individual, based on his or her preferred behavioral style.

The framework of behavioral styles I will use in this book are based on the work of William Moulton Marston and are often referred to as the DISC model of human behavior. Marston described these four behavioral styles in his 1928 book, *Emotions of Normal People.* Since then, the framework has been further refined to reflect a two-axis, four dimensions depiction of behavioral styles: Dominance, Influence, Steadiness, and Conscientiousness. Marston himself never developed an instrument or assessment tool to measure behavior. Later authors and researchers expanded on his model and developed a variety of applications and assessments, including the DISC framework.

DISC Framework

The DISC framework is based on the degree to which an individual views his or her circumstances, or frame of reference, as favorable or unfavorable. A favorable frame of reference reflects the belief that one operates within a supportive environment where he or she can feel comfortable. An unfavorable frame of reference reflects a belief that one operates within an antagonistic environment and he or she feels challenged by these forces. This is the first principle.

The individual's behavioral response to the situation depends on how much power the person feels in relation to the supportive or antagonistic forces in the environment. For example, if I perceive myself as more powerful, I will act on the environment to achieve my purpose. If I perceive myself as less powerful, I will accommodate to the environment. This is the second principle.

These two principles intersect to produce four responses directed by emotions (four behavioral styles):

Dominance **(Profile #1)** acts on an environment perceived as unfavorable to the self.	**Influence** **(Profile #2)** acts on an environment perceived as favorable.
Conscientiousness **(Profile #4)** accommodates to an environment perceived as unfavorable.	**Steadinessness** **(Profile #3)** accommodates to an environment perceived as favorable.

Individuals tend to use two of these four preferred behavioral styles, a primary style and secondary style. Since these are behavioral styles, everyone is capable of using all four styles, though for some, a particular style may be seen as a "learned behavior" and therefore the person may feel awkward when using these behaviors. Though all combinations are possible, common combinations include: Dominance-Influence; Dominance-Conscientiousness; Steadiness-Conscientiousness; and Influence-Steadiness.

Uses of the Behavioral Styles Framework

The DISC framework seeks to explain how people relate to one another. Typical applications include team building, management development, sales training, and persuasive communication messaging. The common approach to understanding the behavioral styles and applying their insights is:

1. Recognize your own preferred style(s) and the impact your behavior has on others;
2. Recognize the style preference of the person you are interacting with;
3. "Flex" to match the style of the other person – to speak their language

The next four sections go into greater detail on each of the four behavioral styles, including their preferred way of doing and communicating.

A final note. These are not clinical tools to understand people's psyches and such applications are strongly discouraged by the professional community. In addition, these assessment tools have limited value as predictors of performance when it comes to evaluating job candidates and should be used only after a candidate has been selected.

Dominance Style – In Detail

G iven that the Dominance style (D) is described as acting on an environment perceived as unfavorable to the self, it's no wonder the key to understanding D-style people is to remember it's all about *progress*, moving things forward. If someone perceives themselves as more powerful than the forces in their environment, they are naturally inclined to take action. Combine that with their assessment that they need to counteract the unfavorable environment and you get a person who only knows one direction – forward – and one orientation – proactive.

Armed with this insight, it's logical that a D-style person prefers to:

Get to the point. Any conversation deemed extraneous to the task at hand is going to be undervalued, and even disparaged, by a D-style person. "Don't dance around an issue, give it to me straight" – otherwise they start thinking you're wasting valuable time, attention, and effort – all of which could be better spent in taking action, making decisions, or addressing roadblocks. In a similar vein, they usually want to hear about an issue, problem or project by *starting at the end first*. Starting at the beginning of the story, in a logical, sequential fashion, sends huge warning signals to a D-style person because he or she knows that you will end up providing too much information and will overload the issue. They want the bottom line first and then will ask you for the background information, *if* they feel they need it. If they don't ask for it and you feel compelled to share all the information with them, know that you are potentially putting yourself on thin ice. As soon as they determine you are slowing them down, you are sinking fast.

Make decisions. Decisions represent making progress to the D-style person. They may not be the best decisions or ones based on complete data but they do represent the best choice, given what's known at the time. They will ask direct questions to get to information that will help them make the best decision possible, such as asking someone for his or her opinion or judgment on an issue or other individual. These questions can often come across as fairly blunt, potentially putting some people in an awkward situation of giving their opinion of a failing project or under-performing colleague. But the D-style person rarely attaches any personal harm to the question or answer. Rather, their view is often "we don't have time for playing nice. We've got a job to get done." Their refined ability to assess risk in the moment should not be under-estimated. They make a clear distinction between reckless and risky. Reckless is what they did in their younger days; risk management is what they do everyday. They believe whether a decision is ultimately viewed as good or bad depends a great deal on whether it is delivered in the optimal window of opportunity – both time and circumstances. Delay a decision too long and the opportunity spoils or disappears.

Be challenged. If someone is predisposed to act on an environment perceived as unfavorable to them, they're bound to love a challenge – and that's the case with D-style people. Otherwise, they get bored and unoccupied. And once that happens, watch out. "Idle hands are the work of the devil" comes to mind. It's all about "staying fresh by staying challenged." Therefore they love to seek out challenges and to be challenged by others. And not just in areas they have expertise in, which often don't feel challenging enough to them. To use an analogy, push them off a cliff even if they don't know how to swim. They believe, in the 2.3 seconds between the moment you push them off and the moment they hit the water, they will figure out how to swim. One of the best ways to motivate them is to tell them "this is an impossible task for anyone to accomplish" and then delegate it to him or her. They will jump at the opportunity. Just don't slow them down with questions like "how do you plan on accomplishing it?" "TBD," is all they can tell you.

D-style tendencies also include:

- A low tolerance for brainstorming. At some point it begins to feel like a circular conversation going nowhere fast.
- Expecting each person they work with to take responsibility for getting things done (no excuses, no surrender).
- Hiring self-starters and go-getters who don't require a lot of attention or support.
- Switching jobs or leaving an organization, not because of pay issues or a lousy boss, but because they get bored in any position after a certain amount of time (usually around 18 months).
- Stepping into a project and making decisions about next steps if they conclude the project is not moving fast enough – and not just with projects they are responsible for.
- Openness to taking a circuitous route to accomplish something, as long as THEY ARE MOVING!

Style in Action

For a number of years when I lived in Chicago, one of my clients was located in the far northern suburbs. Coming from where I lived in the city, I had the option of taking the freeway route or a surface street route, which wound its way through the lakefront suburban communities with an average posted speed limit of 35 miles per hour and few traffic lights. The freeway route was often congested and prone to significant delays because of traffic accidents. Of the two routes, which one would be the preferred route of a D-style person? Answer: It depends…on time of day, weather conditions, importance of arriving at the destination at a particular time, degree of "stuckness" the D-style person has experienced so far that day. He or she instinctively factors all of this into his or her choice of route. Their choice may not appear logical (out-of-the-way, lower speed limits, etc.) because it's not necessarily about directness or speed. It's all about moving forward.

Influence Style – In Detail

G iven the Influence style is described as acting on an environment perceived as favorable, no wonder people with a preference for the Influence-style view the world as their oyster. They are the most enthusiastic of all the four styles and feed off of positive energy. Therefore the key to understanding and interacting with Influence-style people is *passion*. Show it, express it, look for it, expect it. It's not as though an Influence-style person will be on a constant high, 24 hours a day. But they will look for and respond positively to a sense of energy (positive of course).

Armed with this insight, it's logical that an Influence-style person prefers to:

Look for the positive. Influence-style people are often accused of being natural spinmeisters because they are always putting the positive spin on ostensibly gloomy situations. But they don't see it as conjuring up the positive out of nothing; they see it as pulling out the positive that's already there. They know a positive viewpoint opens up a lot more opportunities to see things in a different light. Influence-style people have learned that perception plays a big role in whether a project is hugely successful or a disaster. It's because how one perceives the situation will influence their attitude about the situation. Once a negative attitude sets in, it's that much more difficult to dislodge it and replace it with a more positive attitude. Influence-style people know that energy and attitude go hand-in-hand – positive energy follows a positive attitude and vice versa. And positive energy directly affects productivity, creativity, innovation, and teamwork. So really, it's not about touchy-feely stuff, it's about getting the job done with the biggest possible impact. That's why they work hard to set the right tone from the very beginning and attend to things that will keep the energy and positive attitude growing.

Work with others. Influence-style people gravitate towards group efforts for many reasons. One, they know the right mix of people and talents can translate into extraordinary results unattainable by any one individual. Two, it gives them the opportunity to feed off the enthusiasm and energy of other people, which is hugely motivating to them. Three, they know the quality of ideas and effort goes way up when the right teamwork generates a certain kind of electricity by exchanging and building on one another's ideas. They believe this group dynamic has the advantage of generating ideas of high quality <u>and</u> quantity. And besides, it's fun! What could be better than to experience or witness the spark of ideas among a group of people? Influence-style people do so in the name of having a greater impact on the task, the people, the company, the customer, or even the world. No wonder Influence-style people believe the greatest effort should aim for the greatest impact and that can only be done collectively. Otherwise why put all that time and energy into achieving average results?

Attract attention. If you want to have an impact on the world around you, why wouldn't you make sure people know what you are capable of accomplishing? It's a sure way to keep opportunities coming your way that will help you make your mark. That's how an Influence-style person sees it. There's so much to accomplish and so little risk in the favorable environment, it's only logical to jump in with a grand entrance, as they will tell you. And with all this goodwill floating around, no wonder Influence-style people treat others as his or her "new best friend." Admittedly all of this requires a certain amount of "tooting one's horn" but for a good cause – it's usually more about "put me to work where I can make a difference" and less about "put me on a pedestal." Whether it be through their wardrobe, personality, or extroverted nature, Influence-style people seek to be noticed for the greater good. This can include creating an opportunity to connect with another person or showing others all the great things they have to offer. But ultimately, the primary reason is for them to have the most positive impact possible.

Influence-style tendencies also include:

- Needing the spotlight on a regular basis.
- Engaging in social conversations before launching into the work.
- A willingness to engage in potentially conflictual discussions if they feel the unresolved issues are undermining the working relationship.
- Finding ways to combine work with fun.
- Making conscious, concerted efforts to change negative attitudes of others.
- Avoiding too many facts or details, lest they paint too much of a negative picture or distract people from their vision.

Style in Action

A few years ago a friend of mine was living in Washington, D.C. working as a temp, driving a shuttle bus between two locations for one of the federal agencies. He took the subway to work and noticed after a few days another gentleman got off at the same subway stop, walked over to the same location, boarded his bus and never once said a word to my friend. The lack of interpersonal connection (through a simple "how are you?" or "good morning") was unacceptable to my friend, as he himself said as he told me the story. He "vowed" to change the situation and establish some sort of connection. So little by little, day-by-day, my friend tried a variety of conversation starters. And sure enough, he succeeded in opening up the lines of communication with the passenger. However, the reason for my friend relating this story to me was now he couldn't get the guy to shut up during the trips...yap, yap, yap all the way there, the same the way back. A fairly common dilemma for the Influence-style person – "we've made a connection and now they won't leave me alone!"

Steadiness Style – In Detail

The Steadiness style (S) is described as accommodating to an environment perceived as favorable. This implies S-style people perceive themselves as less powerful and therefore accommodate to the environment. But this does not mean that S-style people see themselves as power*less*. Rather, they recognize at some level that there are a number of reasons, beyond their control, for why someone might have more power than they do, such as level of authority; 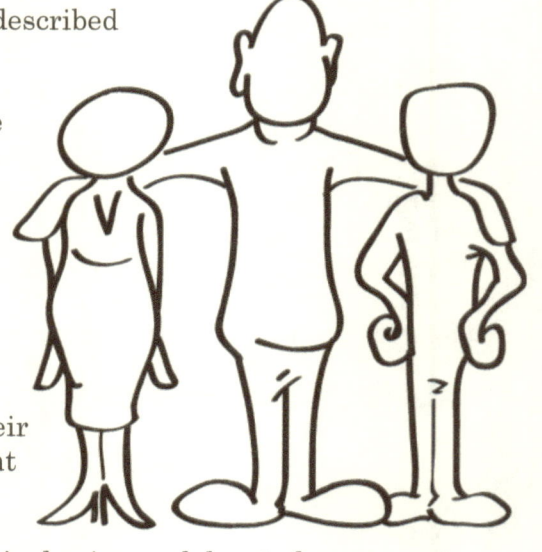 more information about a particular issue; delegated power as in a democratic process; or personal charisma. But since they view their environment as favorable, they naturally look there for sources of power beyond themselves, such as strength in numbers and power of consensus. Therefore they view social groups as sources of power, not to be used to dominate but to bring about desired results. The key to understanding and interacting with S-style people is to understand their view of *power* and how they go about compensating for their self-perception as less powerful through their membership in cohesive, strong social groups.

Armed with this insight, it's logical that an S-style person prefers to:

Avoid conflict. Disagreements pose a threat to the cohesiveness of a group and undermine the ability to reach consensus. Rather than confront an issue head-on with the party involved, an S-style person is more likely to seek first to reach some sort of understanding or compromise with the other party. But this version of accommodating is often mistaken by others as passive, even submissive, behavior. The S-style sees this trait very differently. They hear the words "yield," "make concessions," "strike a balance," "harmonize," "meet halfway," "adapt," and "reconcile" and think "active engagement with the other party." In fact, where others would argue compromise means neither party gets what they want, an S-style person sees compromise in its original meaning – to promise together. This mutuality is at the heart of the S-style approach to addressing conflict: discover our commonality rather than accentuating what divides us. Though they recognize that they are prone to yield or make concessions when in a conflict situation, they would strenuously disagree that their behavior reflects surrendering, deserting one's principles, evading or ducking responsibility, or a cop out. They acknowledge conflict is a fact of life but would rather find ways to lessen its disruptive effect on a group or relationship.

Maintain a high level of personal competency and ability. S-style people look to balance their personal need to gain a degree of individual power over their situation with maintaining the supportive forces in their environment. They don't want to be seen as overstepping their boundaries or even worse, as aggressive. Therefore they often focus their efforts on developing their expertise and knowledge as sources for personal power. This makes sense, given two other sources of power, reward and coercion, typically pit one individual or group against another. The idea that someone would manipulate a person or group in such a manner causes great consternation in an S-style person. They work hard to keep their skills relevant to their responsibilities and seek out feedback regularly to ensure they are on the right track. Being seen as competent and a contributor to the group's success has two rewards. It strengthens their perception of personal power while at the same time strengthens their social power through the team's cohesiveness and ability to produce. What complicates this seemingly win-win arrangement is the pace of change in today's companies and increasingly global economy. Rarely does an individual have the luxury of preparing for a change months in advance. More often it feels like "starting tomorrow..." which leaves the S-style person scrambling to figure out what they will need to be able to do in the new world to remain competent. If they determine they will need a new skill set, they can begin to panic if there isn't sufficient amount of time for them to upgrade their expertise or knowledge. That's why others often perceive the S-style as being resistant to change. They can't help but put some sort of brakes on the change or their source of personal power will be undermined.

Observe before expressing. That which we lack we often study. So is the case with S-style people when it comes to power. They have learned the value of sitting back and observing what people say and don't say and what actions are taken and not taken. Then they will offer their own opinion or ideas. An S-style person is a realist when it comes to group power and politics. Therefore they seek to understand the dynamics of a situation and incorporate as much of their knowledge, expertise, awareness, and data in order to gain as complete of a picture as possible. Only then do they feel they have a clear understanding of the landscape (with its landmines) they will need to navigate through. In this sense, they are "full picture" versus "big picture" thinkers. Their assessment of a situation has a 3-D quality to it – past, present, and future when it comes to players, politics, expectations, accomplishments, and failures. If you really want to know what's really going on in the company, ask an S-style person (offline and in confidence).

S-style tendencies also include:

- Being viewed by their peers as an informal leader because of their integrity, longevity, and humility.
- Avoiding situations where their individual accomplishments are publicly recognized, separate from the team.
- Seeking as much information as possible about the what, why, when, where, and how of an announced change.
- Thoroughly exploring all possible ideas until consensus is reached.
- Long term employment with one company because longevity confers advantages when it comes to expertise and knowledge as to "how things work around here."
- Taking a measured, thoughtful approach to what they say in a group setting.

Style in Action

One of my first clients after starting my consulting practice was the leadership team of a religious community. I was invited by a member of the team to help them address some issues they were struggling with, specifically their ability to surface and discuss sources of potential conflict.

Being less wise, I approached the issue as I saw best ... get the issues out on the table and address them one by one directly, like adults. Much to my surprise, when I went around the table and asked each leadership team member why they felt the team avoided conflict, most found a way not to answer the question – either by pausing long enough for someone else to step in or by painting the issue in a more positive light: "It's not so much we avoid conflict as we could do a better job of feeling comfortable with the idea of conflict." Sounded like the same thing to me.

It was only later when I learned about the notion of behavioral styles that I could see the errors of my way. My approach to surfacing potential conflict was much too direct for this team, which was probably made up of several S-style individuals. I had to find a different way for the team members to voice their concerns in a safe environment that protected their identity and preserved their social relationships. How did I do it? By having one-to-one conversations, assembling everyone's comments, scrubbing the comment of any personal identity and feeding back to the team a summary of what I heard. From there we were able to move to "now what?" as compared to dealing with the usual posturing that comes with a high S-style team trying to deal with conflict. This approach turned "personality clashes" into a form of data that gave everyone just enough emotional distance to be able to work on the real issues. It took a bit more time but with a bigger payoff of less dancing around the issues and more time addressing them.

Conscientiousness Style – In Detail

The Conscientiousness style (C) is described as accommodating to an environment perceived as unfavorable. This would imply C-style people perceive themselves as less powerful. But as I mentioned in "Meaning Behind the Behavior," "the individual's behavioral response to the situation depends on how much power the person feels *in relation* to the supportive or antagonistic forces in the environment." This is a critical distinction to make when it comes to understanding the C-style, because for the most part, they are secure in the supremacy of their source of personal power – their knowledge and expertise. This self-assessment has far less to do with ego and more to do with homework. The C-style person works very hard to know as much as they can about an issue or topic and to think through as thoroughly as possible all the implications and angles to come up with a bullet proof game plan. Combined with an orientation that strives for ever-higher standards of excellence, a C-style person often feels empowered when their hard work proves to them that "right" is on their side.

So why would they perceive themselves as less powerful *in relation* to the antagonistic forces in the environment? Because they see themselves as severely outnumbered by people willing to get things done by cutting corners or lowering standards – the people willing to settle for something less than perfect. These people are the embodiment of the antagonistic forces. The key, then, to understanding the C-style is *perfection*. Striving for perfection fuels their source of personal power (knowledge and expertise) and allows them to make a significant contribution to a disorganized and shoddy world they see around them. In their minds, it is a never-ending battle against the forces of mediocrity.

Armed with this insight, it's logical that a C-style person prefers to:

Establish and follow standard operating procedures (SOP's). If one is attempting to assert one's high standards on an uninterested, if not antagonistic, audience, it makes sense to work to set up procedures or a process that all parties agree to follow. Creating SOP's imply the various stakeholders buy into the expectations – a common understanding and agreement that everyone commits to following an objective standard. That's why C-style people invest more than others in crafting these SOP's to ensure these group standards reflect, to the greatest extent possible, their own standards. But the ability to influence situations (one definition of personal power) requires more than just a set of agreed-upon expectations of how things will get done. It also calls for holding people accountable for following these SOP's. And that's where a C-style person can be hard to shake off when people start to deviate from the SOP. What others would describe as "extenuating circumstances" or "being responsive to the customer," C-style people see as laziness, laxity, and an undisciplined approach.

Do it right the first time. An off-shoot of the C-style's striving for perfection is their orientation to do the task right the first time. Otherwise the effort reflects sloppy thinking or poor planning and results in wasted mental activity, time, and resources. Therefore, a C-style person will want to thoroughly analyze a situation before taking action. They will want to make sure that every angle and possible alternative has been analyzed, *objectively*, so that they can determine the optimal process or approach they should take to achieve the desired goal, *the first time out*. They recognize the need for testing but view this as something that's done "off line" and does not necessarily reflect a possible version of the final product or service. In other words, testing is exempt from any critique or evaluation; it is a discovery process and should be treated as such by the people who are trying to rush the C-style person and cause them to deliver a substandard output. This attention to getting it right the first time can create the perception in the minds of others that the C-style person is a procrastinator – struggling to come to a conclusion or resolution that would move the project forward. A more accurate critique would be "paralysis by analysis." The C-style person can become so fixated on getting it right the first time that they end up spending far too much time checking every possible data source and conceivable angle. This is particularly problematic when it is a time-sensitive, market-driven project.

Rely on data. C-style people learn early on that people rely far too much on personal opinion when deciding the best course to pursue. And it's very frustrating to argue one's point when the response is "well that's the way I feel." That being the case, the C-style person turns to data as the antidote to personal feelings, but not necessarily because they are a "numbers" person. Data presumes objectivity, which is very attractive to a C-style person, particularly when it comes to dealing with interpersonal conflict over competing ideas. And since data are the basis of logic, any decision-making process that includes as much data as possible is bound to come up with the most logical (and presumably, best) solution. But to deliver its full potential, data have to be organized properly to reveal true insights and answers. Is it no surprise, then, that C-style people tend to habitually turn to spreadsheets to organize their thoughts, data, and decisions. Forced to make a decision on the spot with incomplete data or to share their analysis-in-progress, the C-style person will make it very clear all the caveats involved in the data. They do this as a means of protecting themselves from possible ramifications of others misusing the incomplete data or analysis down the road and linking the poor quality to the C-style originator.

C-style tendencies also include:

- Having extremely high standards for themselves as well as for the people who work for or with them.
- Preferring to have very specific parameters for what is expected of their work.
- Taking a well thought out, methodical approach to getting the job done.
- Emphasizing thoroughness, quality, and correctness in their work and the work of others.

- Taking a "trust but verify" approach when checking the work of others.
- Experiencing higher levels of frustration with situations and/ or people who they see as putting roadblocks in their way of achieving their high standard of perfection.

Style in Action

A few years back, I was facilitating a teambuilding workshop for about twenty people. The room had been set up in a u-shaped layout. During the morning break, I did my customary double-check to ensure all the materials we would be using were there and ready to go. I noticed that the pile of individualized behavioral style reports was out of order so I quickly put them in order.

When we got to the point in the workshop where I would hand out these reports, I naturally handed them out in alphabetical order, how I had organized them. As I was handing the reports out, criss-crossing within the u-shape classroom, I noticed my client, the project manager for this training, looking quite agitated in the back of the room. Unable to come up with an obvious reason for his behavior, I finished handing out the reports and gave the group some time to read them over.

The next thing I know, my client (a C-style person) suddenly appeared next to me and asked in a hush voice, "how did the reports get out of order?" And I said, "they weren't, I corrected them during the break." And he said, "what? I put them in order of where people were sitting so all you had to do was hand the pile of reports to the person on the end of the u-shape and each person's report would be on top as they passed the pile around the room." He was right, his order was logical *and* efficient – a thing of beauty. I could tell my apology was irrelevant in his eyes. His words said "no problem" but his eyes said "next time, don't mess with my order."

In Their Own Words: D-style person

Note: since these are actual transcripts (slightly edited) of interviews with real people, these will not be "pure" descriptions of the particular style. You will likely read a comment that sounds more like a different style – a reminder that we are more than just one box on a framework. I have also called-out certain quotes from the interview I think are insightful and noteworthy for understanding and recognizing these style preferences in real people.

Gail

BT: Gail, how best to work with you?

Gail: I think you need to work hard. And you need to demonstrate that you at least will make every attempt to deliver the end goal, in an expeditious, timely manner.

BT: Okay, so it doesn't have to always be fast, fast, fast, but it's definitely got to be timely.

Gail: Well, it doesn't even have to be fast, fast, fast. It has to be in the time in which you said you would meet that end goal. So if you tell me it's going to take a year, fine. But in a year, either it should be done, or you need to demonstrate that you made every possible effort to make it happen. Failure is fine. So if it implodes on itself, but you did everything you could to try and make sure that it works, fine. But you have to demonstrate that you are working at the problem.

BT: Why is that so important to you?

Gail: Because I want to know that someone is working as hard as I am.

BT: So you work pretty hard?

Gail: I would say so.

BT: Next question, if I needed to influence you to my way of thinking, or to at least consider a different way than what you're currently thinking, what would be the best way to influence you?

Gail: Be very direct.

BT: Literally say, "I need to influence you"?

Gail: No, just say that … well, it depends on what you mean by influence. Do you want to express a different opinion than mine?

BT: Yes, but in the hope that you will agree with my opinion. How do I get you to perhaps buy-in to what I am suggesting?

Gail: It depends on whether or not your opinion is good.

Very indicative of a Conscientiousness-style preference

BT: And how do you judge opinions?

Gail: I would say from the data that's presented. If you have a rational argument for why your plan is the better plan, great. You have to come to the table with data. It's not "I feel as if it would work better this way." It has to be a thought-out strategy. It doesn't even have to be long, but you have to have data to suggest that yours is the better option. And if you do, great, then let's go.

BT: Switching topics, how do you like to make decisions?

Gail: With data.

BT: And what if there's incomplete data?

Gail: You have to make the best choice possible. It depends. If a decision does not have to be made immediately, then I'm willing to wait and see if we can get more information. But if we need to make a decision to continue to move on, then you take what's available and you make the best judgment you can. And a lot of times it's based on consensus.

BT: How so?

Indicative of a Steadiness-style preference; in this case it sounds like a Dominance-style who learned the hard way.

Gail: I traditionally will make sure everyone involved in the team is in agreement because it doesn't help if I try and lead the team down a road that they're not bought into.

BT: Is there a typical way that you try to get consensus?

Gail: I ask them their opinion. But I will tell you that I know that that's a difficult thing for some people. They don't like to share their opinion in a group setting, that's difficult for them. I've learned to ask them privately.

Very insightful on her part that she can recognize other styles and looks to adjust to them to accomplish her goal.

BT: But your preferred way would be "we're all in the room together, we've got to work on this, we've got to come to a consensus on this, let's talk about it right now."

Gail: We don't all have to be in the room together, but we do have to get it done when it needs to be done. So, now, does that mean that if someone is out on vacation for four months, am I going to chase them down to try and get the answer? No. But if everyone is available, I will talk to all of them. If we happen to be in a meeting, I'll ask them then, if they're not, I'll make a phone call.

A D-style person is more likely to pick up the phone instead of email in the hopes of reaching the person and getting the issue settled then and there.

BT: How do you like to solve problems? Is there a particular way of going about that?

Gail: I like solving problems immediately. I don't like for them to fester.

BT: What's your worry if they sit there too long?

Gail: I feel bad and I don't want someone else to be feeling bad. Any kind of problem, I'm that way. Personal problems? Absolutely. I will try and fix the problem immediately, because I don't want someone to be feeling negative, because that's unproductive, and

Notice she describes addressing people's feelings in the context of productivity – very much like the Dominance-style.

I don't want them to feel negatively towards me because that would make me sad. My end goal is that everyone be a high functioning team. Now, in a work problem, I try to solve it immediately because I don't like to make mistakes and so if I make a mistake I want to fix it.

BT: Okay, and on the scale of a direct approach to an indirect approach, where would your problem solving approach fit? As you go about addressing a problem, do you tend to take a more direct approach, or a more indirect approach?

Gail: Seventy five percent. Even though I'm direct, I try to be conscientious about what I'm saying to that person. So I will sit there and think "what's the best way?" Obviously, you don't want to antagonize the person. You don't want them to think that you blame them. You want them to help you solve the problem. If you attack them, you've just totally imploded on yourself. So, I try. I'm not necessarily good at it, but I do try.

BT: Along those lines of what you just said, what's your relationship to conflict, or your reaction to it? Is it a big deal for you? How do you view it? Is it something to be avoided?

Gail: It depends on what you mean by that. I hate conflict, personally, which is why I will try and address the problem immediately. The first time I see a potential conflict, I will try and address it, because I just don't like it.

BT: Okay, it's something you don't like, but it doesn't sound like it's something that intimidates you. You're saying, "As I see it, I want to address and take care of it right away."

Contrast this with the Steadiness-style who will try to steer clear of the conflict once they see it.

Gail: Right. What's interesting though, I'm very respectful of the bounds in which I work. So, if this was in the purview of my work, I will have no problem with conflict. If at any point it goes out of my space, that's not my immediate responsibility, then often I won't get involved because it's not my place. That could be the culture I grew up in. You just respect authority. Now of course, I don't always respect authority. I will explain my issues if I disagree with my boss, I will definitely say something if he's made a decision that I don't agree with, but I won't counter him in an external meeting.

BT: You'll talk about it one-on-one, off-line.

Gail: Right.

BT: And when do certain things fall under the category of conflict? Is a disagreement the same thing as conflict in your mind? If we have two different opinions?

Gail: I guess. I don't know. Conflict to me is drama.

BT: So it's a little bit bigger than we have two different opinions.

Gail: Right.

BT: There might be some emotional element to it.

Gail: Right, I don't like that. I don't do well with that.

BT: Emotion.

Gail: No ... I really do feel bad. If someone has a breakdown in front me, I really don't know how to handle that well. Okay, so here's another pattern of my behavior because of the fact I'm very respectful of my boundaries and I'm very dedicated to getting the job done. I will give anyone the chance to work with me. But, if I see that they're not performing up to the level in which I prefer, if I have an opportunity, I will just stop working with them. Does that mean that I will go and complain about them to their supervisor? No, I just won't make use of their services, and I'll just keep going and either do it myself or find some other way to get it done. So then, in that way, it's conflict avoidance because I'm not there to screw up someone else's career.

BT: And I would also take from what you just said that if you're working on a peer-to-peer level, you're not necessarily there to help them get better. You expect them to bring a level of competency to the effort from the beginning.

Gail: If it's peer-to-peer, right. Now, I have no problem mentoring people. But it has to be in a role in which it's evident to me that I am to mentor them. When it comes to a colleague, if they want to be mentored and they ask for my opinion, I'm more than happy to share my opinion with them. But if they don't ask for my opinion, I'm not going to impose my opinion on their behavior. I'm not going to tell someone else how to approach their work, unless they are working for me, or they have asked me for it. So if you and I are working together, and I see you're just not doing what my expectations are, it's not that I'll avoid you, but I won't necessarily ask you to do as much work as I might have on the team. And this is not necessarily good behavior, I recognize that.

BT: Changing to the next topic, how do you like to be communicated with? How best for someone to approach you? And that could be as tactical as do you prefer telephone conversations, email, face-to-face? Or how should I structure my message to you?

Gail: If it's a problem that's bothering you, immediately. The fastest mode of communication is preferred. So if something happens and you're waiting to see me, and you don't see me for three weeks, and then it comes up, I would have preferred either the phone call or the email, just so

> *Versus the most personalized mode, such as face-to-face or telephone call, which would be more of an Influence-style preference.*

that it's not something that's festering for three weeks. And when that communication occurs, it would be "you know, I have this issue." Just come out and say it. I can't stand it if someone's going to dance around an issue. If you dance around the issue, then I just try and help – I'll start to formulate what I think is going to come out of your mouth, which is also very unproductive because sometimes I'm going down the entirely wrong road. So just say it.

BT: Be direct.

Gail: Very direct.

BT: What's the best way to compliment you if I feel you've done something really deserving of praise?

Gail: Wow, I don't know. I don't really like them. I don't really like compliments.

BT: Okay.

Gail: I think probably just respect.

BT: And how would I show respect to you?

Gail: By asking my opinion on things, or including me in important decisions. Making me feel like I'm an integral part of the team, as opposed to a not-so-integral part of the team. I think direct compliments are very ineffective. My philosophy is, if someone always says something positive to you but never says anything negative, then you can't judge the reality of that compliment.

BT: So are you saying that part, at least part, of a way that someone can compliment you is also to give you the negative or constructive feedback?

Gail: Right, but don't always compliment. It can't be 100% of the time. If you're going to compliment, it should be infrequent. Because the more frequent the compliments come, the less value they have.

BT: It sounds like the best way to compliment you is through my actions, rather than through my words.

Gail: Correct.

BT: Put you on projects that are interesting, that really use your skills, to involve you in key decisions, things like that.

Gail: Yes.

BT: Then what's the best way to give you negative feedback?

Gail: To say it.

BT: Just say it?

Gail: Yeah.

BT: And given what you've already said, and just say it directly?

Gail: Yes.

BT: Should I be worried about hurting your feelings?

Gail: Well, I mean, you don't have to be obnoxious about it. It's more like "Look, I've noticed that something is not working and I want to offer you a way in which you might approach it the next time."

BT: Okay.

Gail: And constructive criticism is really valuable.

BT: So that's just not a touchy feely expression to you, constructive criticism. You see that as a very tangible, useful thing.

Gail: Right. But I don't want to hug you after it.

BT: Let's not get crazy here.

Gail: Right, I just want to know, I want to continuously evolve and get better. There's a constant desire to do better. Part of that, the only way you can do better is by feedback. Now, does anyone like getting constructive criticism? Probably not, but it's better to know that someone's telling it to your face rather than telling all the coworkers around you, but not you. That's awful.

BT: What I also heard from that example you gave was it sounds like you'd prefer the feedback to be very specific, situational.

Gail: Right. So this always goes back to the data. There has to be representative examples. Because I like to fix things, the only way you can fix things is to see the examples of "this is the problem" and "this is the suggestion on how you could fix it" along with whatever constructive criticism needs to come with that solution. It doesn't come across as a problem as long as they come to me and say, "Here's the problem and I think we can fix it this way." They have to demonstrate some type of effort to make it better.

> *Giving examples is effective for all styles but notice how she uses the word "data" to describe this – very indicative of a Conscientiousness-style.*

BT: To keep things moving ahead?

Gail: Right.

BT: Next question, if someone needed to delegate something to you, what's the best way to go about it? How would somebody set it up with you so that you received it positively and were able to get the job done. Anything you need in particular from someone delegating to you?

Gail: I just need to know the boundaries in which I am capable of working, and what the expectations are because

> *Very indicative of a Conscientiousness-style.*

I move for a target. As long as I know what the end goal is and where I can work. It's like you're looking at a graphical picture, you need to put a target on one side of the page, and then put two lines

Very indicative of a Dominance-style.

going toward that target saying that I can move anywhere in between those lines. That's my path to get there. I really don't do well if you don't give me boundaries. I really can't stand the kind of person who says, "Oh, just go ahead and do this," and then you cross some invisible line that you didn't know was there, and then they slap your hand. It would have been much more beneficial if you'd just said, "Oh, and you can't do X, Y, and Z."

BT: Excellent. So, how do you tend to handle stress? How would we even tell if you were feeling stressed out at any particular time?

Gail: Oh, I will usually tell you.

BT: So you are fairly open about saying that, maybe not using the word stressed, but conveying it?

Gail: Yes, but you know what, I have a pretty high limit. I usually won't say anything until I'm frazzled. Which is not necessarily healthy, but I will usually take on an amazing amount of burden before I will say something.

BT: Okay. Now when you're reaching your tolerance level, that very high tolerance level, are we seeing an angrier you, a little more clipped conversation?

Gail: Only in the house with my kids. In the work environment, what I'll do is simply say, "Look, we've passed our limit, we can't do anymore." And I'll draw the line. And then, as long as they hear that and we can maintain the current level that we're at, I'm perfectly fine. The problem is when the people you tell that they're overtaxing you, if they don't hear it, then I might, after several times, get a little irritated. But then I'll still just perform at that level. But usually that's because I'm saturated.

BT: Do you tend to try to re-group things, and maybe re-adjust projects, or is it more a "stop putting more stuff on the plate until we get everything done that we currently have on the plate?"

Gail: I usually try to stop putting stuff on the plate, although I'm not very good at it.

BT: But rarely would you try to re-adjust a project to maybe make it more doable, but maybe not as thorough?

Gail: No. I don't like to get involved in something unless I'm going to try and make it really good. So in other words, am I willing to settle on a project? Typically not.

> *She's probably thinking "perfection" but saying "really good" – very indicative of a Conscientiousness-style.*

BT: OK, moving on. What's the best way to motivate you? So if your boss was trying to keep you at that level, what could he or she do to feed that motivation?

Gail: For me, motivation is the personal satisfaction from the accomplishment and the work. So as long as there is evidence of having a successful impact around you, that's one thing. That's the first thing. The second thing is I'm not driven by money. If I'm interested in the work that I'm doing, I will do it. But, the one limit is that I don't like to be taken advantage of. For instance, do I have to be making the most money in the department? No. But if they were to significantly underpay me compared to the rest of the people, that would totally de-motivate me. To me, it's all about fairness. Just treat me fairly and I'm perfectly happy. Do I want to be treated overly fairly? No, I'm uncomfortable in that situation. If for some reason I were getting $50,000 bonuses or something and no one else were, that would make me very uncomfortable. As long as I'm in the mix, great.

BT: So here's our last question. What would you tell somebody is the magical key that would unlock how best to work with you? "If you did this, if you took this approach when working with me, we're going to be pretty good working together."

Gail: If you demonstrate to me that you're conscientious and that you're willing to work hard, that's it.

Sounds like a Dominance-Conscientiousness style combination.

In Their Own Words: I-style person

Note: *since these are actual transcripts (slightly edited) of interviews with real people, these will not be "pure" descriptions of the particular style. You will likely read a comment that sounds more like a different style – a reminder that we are more than just one box on a framework. I have also called-out certain quotes from the interview I think are insightful and noteworthy for understanding and recognizing these style preferences in real people.*

Lori

BT: So Lori, how best to work with you?

Lori: How best to work with me... well, I spent a couple minutes thinking about this. A few things. One of the things is, I like to

be involved in everything that's happening. Not that I need to
know all of the little details, but I feel more comfortable when I
know what everything else is going on in the department. Not
that I want to get involved, but just so that I have a broader
understanding of what's happening, so that maybe I could
figure out a way to pull all of it together at different points.

BT: And how best to keep you involved? Is
it like copying you on emails or can a
newsletter work as well?

> *Influence-style people tend to come across as "big picture" people.*

Lori: Exactly. Yes, just talk to me on email or when we go to lunch,
just sort of bring it up. Involve me
in the planning group meetings
where it's just the little tidbits
of everything that's happening.
Or when a visitor comes to the
department, be sure to introduce
me and let me know who they are and why they're here, like
"this is so and so from this area, they're here to talk about
such-and-such."

> *She assumes she will be having lunch with her colleagues on some sort of regular basis – not every style is that social.*

BT: So if someone was brought into the office space for a meeting
with somebody else, and they didn't bother to introduce you or
even give you a little background on why they're there, that
would bother you?

Lori: Right. I'd just prefer to know.

BT: Next topic, how do you react to conflict? How would you even
define conflict?

Lori: Conflict to me is when there's not open communication both
ways. So if I'm expressing my feelings or ideas, it would be my
expectation that you would at least sit and listen to them and
wait to hear the whole thing rather than cutting people off
and not understanding where they're coming from. And when
that sort of thing does happen to me, I immediately would just

In Their Own Words: I-style person

Note: since these are actual transcripts (slightly edited) of interviews with real people, these will not be "pure" descriptions of the particular style. You will likely read a comment that sounds more like a different style – a reminder that we are more than just one box on a framework. I have also called-out certain quotes from the interview I think are insightful and noteworthy for understanding and recognizing these style preferences in real people.

---------------------------------- **Lori** ----------------------------------

BT: So Lori, how best to work with you?

Lori: How best to work with me... well, I spent a couple minutes thinking about this. A few things. One of the things is, I like to be involved in everything that's happening. Not that I need to know all of the little details, but I feel more comfortable when I know what everything else is going on in the department. Not that I want to get involved, but just so that I have a broader understanding of what's happening, so that maybe I could figure out a way to pull all of it together at different points.

BT: And how best to keep you involved? Is it like copying you on emails or can a newsletter work as well?

> *Influence-style people tend to come across as "big picture" people.*

Lori: Exactly. Yes, just talk to me on email or when we go to lunch, just sort of bring it up. Involve me in the planning group meetings where it's just the little tidbits of everything that's happening. Or when a visitor comes to the department, be sure to introduce me and let me know who they are and why they're here, like "this is so and so from this area, they're here to talk about such-and-such."

> *She assumes she will be having lunch with her colleagues on some sort of regular basis – not every style is that social.*

BT: So if someone was brought into the office space for a meeting with somebody else, and they didn't bother to introduce you or even give you a little background on why they're there, that would bother you?

Lori: Right. I'd just prefer to know.

BT: Next topic, how do you react to conflict? How would you even define conflict?

Lori: Conflict to me is when there's not open communication both ways. So if I'm expressing my feelings or ideas, it would be my expectation that you would at least sit and listen to them and wait to hear the whole thing rather than cutting people off and not understanding where they're coming from. And when that sort of thing does happen to me, I immediately would just

shut down.
I would
think that
if you
don't feel

> *Very important to understand the circumstances that would lead an Influence-style person to shut down – this drastic shift in behavior can confuse people who work with this style.*

that what I'm saying has value then maybe I don't need to say anything. Maybe I don't need to involve you in anything that I do.

BT: So I might find that, generally speaking, that you're outgoing, very interactive in conversations. Then all of the sudden I might see you shut down. Could that be because you're feeling like your ideas are not being considered by either me or other people?

Lori: Absolutely. Absolutely.

BT: And would that be one of those situations where we would see the most obvious behavioral change in you, or are there other situations where you would not be your usual self because of the circumstances?

Lori: No, I think that would be one of the only. For the most part, I like to be involved in everything to know what's happening. I want to involve everybody unless there's a conflict, like a teammate who's not playing fairly or who is not pulling their weight. It's that sort of thing that would irritate me enough that I would need to stop and somehow explain to them that what they are doing is not okay.

BT: You would find a way to bring it up to them?

Lori: Absolutely.

BT: Let's use a peer-to-peer situation. What are some tactics that you have used in the past to try and bring it up to them, that they're not carrying their weight, for example.

Lori:　I would sort of nicely inquire if there's a task that hasn't been done or if a project is not getting started. I can sort of nicely ask in the beginning, "How's it going? Is there something I can help you with to get it moving?" And then if that still didn't work, then it would be more of a direct face-to-face statement, "It's going to be difficult for me to get my part done if your stuff doesn't get done."

> *Notice how she would start with more of an Influence, indirect approach, and if that doesn't work, is comfortable in taking a more direct approach characteristic of the Dominance-style.*

BT:　So you don't mind being direct when you've made other attempts?

Lori:　Right, and especially if it's going to impact something that I am responsible for, absolutely. I'm not going to look bad because somebody else isn't doing their job.

BT:　Okay, let me change topics. What's the best way to give you negative feedback?

Lori:　I would like honesty and clarity. I don't like just random "Well your results weren't what we wanted." I like to know why. Was it the approach that I took? Was it the delivery? Was it that I didn't involve enough people? I'd like to know specifics so I can actually make the changes to correct them. And I'd like to know when I'm in the middle of the process. I don't like to wait until the very end of the project and have somebody say, "That didn't go how we would have liked." I like regular feedback, such as check-in meetings so I can share "this is my approach, this is how things are moving forward." At that point, if something isn't clear, right then is the best time so I can make changes and finish it properly.

BT:　If I heard you correctly, one of the ways to give you negative feedback is to bring the little things to your attention immediately so you can correct your approach in real time.

Lori: Absolutely. Perfect.

BT: Through regular check-in's – feedback in the moment of "I don't know if that's working well." Is that true?

Lori: Yes.

BT: Excellent. Then what's the best way to delegate to you?

Lori: I don't mind in the moment, we're sitting in a planning meeting and "this needs to be this, this, and this." All at once is fine. I don't like being delegated things after they're already delayed and behind, meaning that if somebody already dropped the ball and the customer is ticked off at that point and then I get the assignment. I then feel the pressure that my results aren't going to be perfect because I didn't have it from the get-go. So I want it right up front. And it doesn't matter how many things, or the depth of things, or the time commitment of it, but as long as it's from the initial stage, I can run with it.

BT: Then what's the best way to motivate you? What keeps you energized, that people can use to motivate you?

Lori: I like to hear "You're doing a great job. I can't believe you got all of this done." I like to be rewarded with more challenges. I like to hear people say, "Wow, we didn't expect that you'd be able to do that, do you think you could expand on it from here?" I really like, "We think you have the potential to do this, so we want to send you to different training classes to learn something new." That is a reward to me, somebody would think I had the potential to learn more and go beyond my education.

BT: It just doesn't have to be compliments, it can be investing in you.

Lori: Yes.

BT: And how do you tend to handle stress? Under what circumstances would we see Lori stressed out?

Lori: I don't think you would see Lori stressed out. My family would see that. It's not something that my friends or coworkers would see. Now if you asked my husband, you'd get a whole different answer. I think it's just part of my personality that I'm supposed to make everything look really easy and that it's not bothering me. What you don't see is when I leave work and go home and I put on my comfy clothes and stay up until midnight getting something done. Or I get up at 6 AM to relieve stress for a couple hours, because you wouldn't see that.

> *Outward appearances tend to be more important to Influence-style people than the other styles.*

BT: Okay, excellent. Next topic. How best to influence you? Let's say I'm working with you as a peer and I want to get your buy-in to an idea that I have. What's going to be a better way for me to get your buy-in?

Lori: I guess involve me in the decision making-process, lead me into where you're going. I want to be part of it, so don't tell me all of the fine details. Rather, approach me with an idea. "Let's think about what if we did something like this." And together we'll work on it until it comes to fruition.

> *This sounds like the Conscientiousness-style may not be one of her preferred styles.*

BT: So you don't need to see something all the way thought through and packaged and ready for your review. You can see something a little bit in the early stages.

Lori: In the early stages I don't need to see any of the details. I can see the broader picture up front, I need to be part of the end result and I need to know the outcome of it. But I don't need to be part of every single little detail.

BT: Now, when you have been forced into those situations of having to be really into the details, is that a pleasant experience or unpleasant?

Lori: You know, it's sometimes different. It's not something I look for, but if it's part of it, it just has to be done. That's the stuff where you just sit down and you give yourself a couple hours and you just knock out the results. But I wouldn't spend a lot of time on details, that's the kind of stuff where I just buckle down and say, "Cover all the details right now and get them done," after I've sat for a couple hours and thought about the process. There's not a lot of time spent on it.

Very characteristic of the Influence-style – not so with either the Steadiness or Conscientiousness-styles

BT: Changing subjects, what's the best way to compliment you?

Lori: In front of other people, publicly; giving me letters, with a picture; in meetings where the rest of our team is there, in introductions with other people, not just "this is Lori" but "this is Lori who takes care of such-and-such, or who did this, or who did that," specific things. Acknowledging loyalty or time commitments that I've put into different arenas as well.

BT: So it would be a big deal if I introduced you to somebody to say all the work you did in your previous position and the work that you're doing now with the department. That history.

Lori: Absolutely.

BT: Would you say you have a particular way of solving problems? How do you go about solving problems?

Lori: Maybe not a particular way. For some problems if they have a quick and easy solution, I'd rather just find the quick way and do it, rather than making a mountain out of a molehill. For example, if there are little things going wrong in the office, like the printer doesn't work and I know that I can either go over and give it a kick right now for an immediate fix versus trying to figure out what's wrong with it and whether we need to order another part, I usually go for the quick fix. On bigger picture things, I like to sit back and think for awhile. I don't necessarily have to sit at my desk and do that. You might think that I'm not working on it, but if I go to lunch with a friend, or I drive my daughter to volleyball, it's going through my mind on ways to solve these things.

BT: Would you say that you have a particular decision making style? How do you like to go about making decisions?

Lori: I like to make decisions that benefit the most people. I like situations where you and I are both gaining something. It doesn't always happen that way. Sometimes I come off more aggressive and that's not the outcome that I like, but in my personal life and my work life, I think that we should all be getting something from the relationship and every decision should have winners on both ends. But not always. If there's definitely a right and wrong, or there can only be one winner, then of course my decision switches over to what's the best way for me to win. And that's usually by being aggressive, or staying up longer, or working harder, or getting it done faster.

See how someone whose preferred styles are Dominance and Influence can go from people focused to task focused?

BT: Did you just use the word "aggressive?"

Lori: Yeah.

BT: So you are capable of being aggressive?

Lori: Absolutely.

BT: Does that sometimes send off mixed signals, because on one hand you're a very pleasant person, very energetic and so forth, and then we see another side? Or do you hide it pretty well?

Lori: I don't think I hide it, but I don't think aggression is necessarily a bad thing. I don't do it with anger, I do it more animated and more energetic. Almost like a team leader ... like a team member on a basketball team. It's sort of aggressive, but more about pulling in the other people around me to do it. Being loud and assertive but in a funny kind of "Come on, be part of it, let's do it. We can do it!" way. That sort of aggressive, not mean.

BT: So more motivating and showing that passion.

Lori: Yeah, passionate. Yeah, enthusiastic.

BT: So how do you like to be communicated with? Do you prefer face-to-face, email, or a particular way of communicating?

Lori: Face-to-face would always be my first choice. It's not always realistic. Email is fine. Email after hours, or if somebody's busy doing something. But if you're going to send emails, then I would expect that at some point there would be face-to-face communications. When I'm meeting with people, I'd much rather go to their office and meet with them than talk on the phone.

BT: Why do you think you prefer more face-to-face? What does that provide you?

Lori: I can see their body language. I can see their facial expressions. I can see if they're rushed, or if they're really into what I'm talking about. I think a lot of people sort of sugar coat and say what they think you want to hear. If you're actually looking at somebody you can read them and tell if they're really into it or not. Then it gives me a baseline for how much I want to involve that person in what I'm doing.

BT: It sounds like once you have that information, you can re-strategize in the moment as to how you're approaching them.

Lori: Yes, totally.

BT: Where do you find most people misunderstand you?

Lori: I think sometimes I come off as flighty and charming and that I just want to have fun. I get that a lot, where people think that I'm here more to just have a good time. Maybe that's because I'm willing to do the work at other times or at a different pace. I think that by not allowing people to see me stressed or really buckling down to do things, they don't see all the hard work, they don't see the late nights and the sweats. But I think that sort of gets me in trouble. I think people look at me and think, "Oh, she's just worried how she looks and about having a good time and about what her kids are doing" but they don't see the commitment to the other work-related things.

BT: So to wrap up, what would you consider to be an inside scoop about how to work with you, that most people wouldn't know about you? Something like the key to understanding how you like to do things? If you could tell them one thing, what would it be?

Lori: Let's see. The understanding that I have very high standards of performance and that I expect other people do as well. And that I actually become de-motivated with people with lower standards or who aren't as motivated to the cause, or the mission as I am. When you come to me to involve me in stuff, be passionate about what you're doing, be energetic. Want to be part of it. If you come to me and you're sending signals that it's just another job, it just completely de-motivates me, I wouldn't want to work with somebody in that situation.

> *Doesn't necessarily mean she has a C-style preference... "high standards" could refer more to what she describes in the next sentences.*

In Their Own Words: S-style person

Note: since these are actual transcripts (slightly edited) of interviews with real people, these will not be "pure" descriptions of the particular style. You will likely read a comment that sounds more like a different style – a reminder that we are more than just one box on a framework. I have also called-out certain quotes from the interview I think are insightful and noteworthy for understanding and recognizing these style preferences in real people.

Doug

BT: Doug, how best to work with you?

Doug: Really, kind of stand-offish. For example, if I'm working on a project, or a project is assigned to me, give me the ultimate goal of what the outcome needs to be. Maybe give me some guidance of where to start, and then I want to take it from there. Typically, I'm a person that can learn from just doing it, rather than someone telling me what to do. But, also on the flip side of that, I want to get ongoing feedback. So, for example, if I'm working on a project that's an eight week project, I like to sit down with my manager or peer and meet on a weekly basis, kind of update, and if we're not where we want to be then I want some open and honest feedback and communication.

An S-style person would say this because of the importance he or she attaches to being a contributing member of any team, department, or company they belong to.

BT: So you like to have that feedback in real time, so that you can make any adjustments?

Doug: Exactly.

BT: You had mentioned feedback. What's the best way to give you negative feedback if someone feels like your performance isn't where it needs to be?

Doug: I prefer honest feedback, just say it how it is because I struggle sometimes to read between the lines. I just want it open, honest, and direct. Not kind of wishy-washy communication, just give it to me how it is. "So Doug, you're not performing up to par. You didn't accomplish this by this time frame." You know, just direct.

BT: Then what would be the best way to compliment you?

Doug: For me, just a simple "great job, keep up the good work," little simple words drive me.

BT: So if I was to do something with the goal of motivating you, are employee awards going to be motivating to you?

Doug: Oh, yeah, absolutely.

BT: How about if you're named employee of the month and you get up in front of your peers and are handed a plaque.

Doug: No. I don't like that attention from my peers.

BT: Oh...

Doug: Yeah, that's one of my things. To be honest with you, I like it, I just don't like it in front of everybody. I just don't want all the attention. But if you give me an award, between me and my boss, then that goes a long way and that's definitely a motivator for me.

A key difference between the S and I-style – how much public recognition.

BT: Okay, but if I was to give the recognition to you in front of your peers, why would that be a de-motivator, what would be going through your head?

Doug: I wouldn't say it's a de-motivator, I just don't like being put up on that pedestal. Don't get me wrong, it's motivating that I got the attention and all that, and I don't want to say I get embarrassed when I'm in front of all these people, it's just that I don't like that kind of attention, I guess.

BT: And how best to influence you? So if I want to get on your good side, what would be some ways that I could do that?

Doug: Positive attitude would be what comes to my mind. I definitely like working with people that are positive. Not the ones who look at everything negatively. So I would say, just positive thinking and positive attitude.

BT: Then how would you define conflict? What would be an example of what you would consider to be a situation with conflict that you might find yourself in?

Doug: Good question. I guess just a disagreement on a point of view, or on part of a project. If I'm stuck on one decision, and I've got someone on the other side that's stuck on their side of the decision and we can't come to a common ground, then I would say that's conflict.

BT: And does that happen frequently?

Doug: No, I wouldn't say it happens frequently, but it seems like I always cave in easier than the other side.

BT: So you may not get very far in that conflict, you might give in sooner?

Key insight into the S-style when it comes to conflict ... just because they are agreeing with you doesn't mean they agree with you.

Doug: Yeah, I would give in sooner just so we could move on.

BT: And in general, how do you feel about conflict? Is it something that you're very comfortable with or that you try to avoid?

Doug: No, I'm comfortable with it. Not everyone likes conflict but if it bothers me, it doesn't bother me for long and I move on. I just try not to let it get to me. I try to come to a quick resolution. I always try to resolve it and get it done, and for that to happen usually I need to cave in and go with the other side of the view, I guess.

BT: Even though you might still think your way is the better way?

Doug: I guess it depends on the situation, but yeah.

BT: Then how do you like to make decisions?

Doug: Fact based decisions. I like to get other people's opinions. I like to get other people's opinions on my decisions, especially my manager. I just feel more comfortable in a decision when

I've got somebody supporting me, supporting my decision. But, really, I try to look at the facts and make the decisions from that. Not by just personal preference.

> *This combination of using facts and soliciting others' opinions would be a common practice of someone whose two strong style preferences are S and C.*

BT: And how would you describe your problem solving process? How do you go about solving problems?

Doug: Again through the fact gathering. Really trying to look at all angles of the problem and getting other opinions, not just my manager, but from my peers too, or people involved on the project. So just in case I'm not seeing something, or someone's seeing something from a different angle. So I always like to get other people's opinions and ponder their thought process, and potentially implement or take their suggestions.

BT: Next question. If I needed to delegate something to you, what would be the best way to delegate it to you?

Doug: I guess just simply email or a "Doug, can you take of this." If I have any questions, then I have to come back, but just a simple "can you take care of this" or "can you work on this."

BT: Let's say it's a project that I know you haven't done before. How would you like me to set you up for success with this new project for you?

Doug: If it was a new project, then I would like to spend maybe 30 minutes or an hour to get the background of the project and what the ultimate goal is and then ask as many questions as possible. And then I would take it from there.

> *In contrast, a D-style person would typically not need to spend as much time getting the background of the project...more likely to jump in and ask questions later.*

BT: And given your answer at the beginning of our conversation, would you want me to schedule regular check-ins, right from the beginning?

Doug: I would probably want to wait on that. If I'm struggling with the project, then I would say let's meet more often. But if it's smooth sailing and it's going well, then there's no point of wasting time, my manager's time or my time for that. And try to get it done as quickly as possible.

> The question to ask Doug is, "are you motivated to get the task done as quickly as possible for the satisfaction that comes with moving things forward or with contributing to the team's productivity?"

BT: How do you tend to handle stress?

Doug: Um, how do I answer this? I'm typically a person that holds it in. I try to move that stress out of the workplace. I guess I do vent it out to my wife. But I try not to vent too much at work.

BT: How would we know at work if you're currently feeling stress? Could we tell by your actions?

Doug: Yeah. I don't smile as much, straight-faced, very quiet. I don't want to say I'm running with my head cut off, but you could tell that my positive attitude diminishes.

BT: But you wouldn't necessarily have a negative attitude?

Doug: No. I would be in a quiet mode.

> Good reminder that "quiet" doesn't reflect everything is OK. If your intuition senses something is troubling the S-style person, ask to speak with him or her privately and outside the view of their colleagues.

BT: So we'd most likely see something different, but nothing really dramatically different.

Doug: No, oh no.

BT:	Then how do you like to be communicated with, in general?

Doug:	I'm easy to approach. I'm really a conversation starter, I'm easy to talk with, approachable.

BT:	Do you have a preference as to face-to-face, telephone, email?

Doug:	To me it doesn't really matter. I love the face time, talking with people. If I would have to rate between the three, I'd prefer face-to-face, number two would be phone, and email would be three. I'm not a big fan of email.

BT:	How come?

Doug:	I think the reason why is, it seems like it takes more time with email and you can get a lot more accomplished with a conversation rather than email. I understand that email is good if you need to document some things, but I just think you can be more productive with a phone call than you can with email.

BT:	What would be the quickest way to tick you off?

Doug:	Not follow through on your commitments or holding up my process. For example, if I'm waiting for something from you, if it's holding me up, and then I get called out on it, such as "Doug wants to delay'" and it's because you didn't get me this information or didn't follow through on your commitments, that would definitely tick me off.

BT:	Would you feel uncomfortable in having to call me out on this to somebody else?

Doug:	No, I would probably say "Brian's promised me this, and I still haven't gotten it." Do I call your name out? I guess it would depend on the situation.

BT:	To confirm, it would make you uncomfortable that you had to say to somebody that you hadn't gotten the job done because you're depending on me.

Doug: Yeah, so here's an example. I was in a meeting this past week and it was on a project I'm a part of and I was still waiting for information from somebody else. It was a round table in front of about 15 people. And I didn't call the person's name because of all the people around, there's no need to drop who was holding up the process, they have a pretty good idea of who it is. But if it was me and my manager speaking, then it would be more likely that I would drop that person's name, call them out.

BT: Now, in this example, was that person in the meeting at that moment?

Doug: No, he was not.

BT: So you didn't bring up the name, but you felt you got across what you needed to.

Doug: Correct.

BT: Excellent. Any other ways to tick you off?

Doug: No, not really, unless someone's getting into my business or someone's commenting on my work, such as "Doug's made the wrong decision" and really not addressing it with me but with everybody else.

BT: So here's the last question. What's one thing that you feel that if we knew about your way of doing things would really help us to understand how best to work with you?

Doug: I guess very approachable and very easy to work with. What I mean by that is if there are issues or things that are going well, I'm definitely approachable on good news and bad news. If I don't have the answer, I'll find the answer. But I'm a person that will work with pretty much anybody.

BT: Do you consider yourself a team player?

Doug: Yes.

BT: How do you typically contribute to that team effort?

Doug: I guess it would matter on a case-by-case situation but if I'm
just in a supporting role, not really somebody who's leading
a team, I can be the fact gatherer or give me a goal or what
needs to be achieved and I'll run with it. But if I'm the leader,
I'm very approachable and easy to work with.

BT: Let's say you were on my team. What if I said, "you're going
to need to present the results of the project to our executive
team." No problem?

Doug: It depends on how well I know everything, the whole subject
matter. I would say for presenting, it depends on who my
audience is. I would be more hesitant to present in front
of the executive board on a relatively new project I'm just
getting familiar with. But on the flip side, I wouldn't have an
issue if I knew the project inside out and had been working
on it for awhile. I would have no problem presenting it to the
executive staff. It would really depend on the knowledge that
I have on the subject.

*Not as motivated by the "thrill" of
a sudden challenge as the D-style
person would more likely be.*

In Their Own Words: C-style person

Note: *since these are actual transcripts (slightly edited) of interviews with real people, these will not be "pure" descriptions of the particular style. You will likely read a comment that sounds more like a different style – a reminder that we are more than just one box on a framework. I have also called-out certain quotes from the interview I think are insightful and noteworthy for understanding and recognizing these style preferences in real people.*

Tim

BT: Tim, how best to work with you?

Tim: If I were to go through and describe that, I think it would basically be, "Oh, just be perfect at everything and just be like me."

BT: And that's an honest answer, right Tim?

Tim: Right. The best way for me to feel like somebody is easy to work with and competent is I can just hand them something and know that it's going to get done and it's going to get done better than I imagined it.

BT: That's a pretty high standard, when you say "better than I imagined it."

Tim: It's a pretty high standard, but it's not like it's an impossible standard. At my previous company, why I enjoyed working there so much was because there were so many people that were that way. And I would say, "Hey, I need your help with this thing. Can you put the other spreadsheet that does whatever?" And then boom, the spreadsheet comes back that's just incredible. Like, "Oh wow, I wouldn't have thought to do it that way. That's awesome. Thank you." It's done. So that's the ultimate, working with folks who can do that. But then I also think about what's the minimal level. And the minimal level is, you have to at least show competence in what you're doing. If you're a bumbling fool, I just can't handle it. And I will either try to not work with you or take the work from you and do it myself, or I will start to micro-manage you.

BT: And how quickly can you size up a person as to where they stand on that range of bumbling idiot to wow?

Tim: It usually takes me a while.

BT: What's a while? Like a day? A month?

Tim: Oh, it takes a lot of trial and error for me. Because I usually assume that people can do it. I don't walk around assuming that everybody is a bumbling fool. So what I'll do is, I'll say, "Hey, can you work on this thing?" and then it will come back and not quite be right, and I'll assume that I've done something wrong with how I explained it. And then, say, "Okay, I wasn't clear. Go off, and here's my new instructions." And then if it comes back again and it's not quite right, it's like "Fool me once, shame on you" kind of thing. So it maybe takes me two or three tries communicating with somebody, having a work product come back, and really trying to figure out if it's me doing something wrong with my communication to them, or if it's them. Then there's all sorts of varying degrees of competence. It might be "Okay, now I realize that you're good at this but not this, so I won't give you any of this kind of stuff anymore." Keep in mind, I'm saying this from a perspective of somebody who is not trying to mentor somebody. If I'm in a position where I'm trying to grow somebody, if they had these shortcomings and I didn't think that they were going to cut it and needed to be fired, then I would explain the areas where I've seen a deficiency and ask for some growth in that area.

BT: What do you mean, ask for some growth? Like, that they take it up a notch?

Tim: Yeah. Take for example if someone was really great at doing all sorts of detailed stuff but were terrible at interacting with clients. Then I would say, "well, you're pretty terrible at interacting with clients. Let's do some practice rounds with these kinds of things. Let's send you to some facilitation training. I'll come to meetings with you while you interact." So there has to be some amount of expertise to make it kind of worthwhile to build out the other areas.

BT: Now something you just said, would you be that direct with someone to say, "You know, you're pretty terrible at the client interaction stuff?"

Tim: I would say it much nicer but definitely, I would be that direct, especially with the people who work for my company because

I want people to be the best of the best when it comes to this stuff. So if somebody had an area they were soft on, I would probably give them the old compliment sandwich: focus on how good they are at these other things and explain it from a behavioral standpoint, "I've seen you do these kinds of things, I've seen these things happen." Not "you are this way," or "you think this way," or "you're terrible," or "you're no good." More like "when we were in this client situation you said this offensive thing and you should not say this offensive thing," something like that. [laughs] I try to give a lot of examples when I give that kind of feedback. I wouldn't want to go into a conversation like that unprepared and not be able to back up my perspective on where I think there's a growth area.

Best of the best – pretty high standard.

BT: So now let's take it to a peer-to-peer perspective. If I were trying to influence you to buy into my idea, what would be the strategy I would need to use?

Tim: I'd say it's all kind of logic and reason. When I'm presented with a decision to be made, what I want to do is research it to the nth degree, to know that I'm making the right decision. Some of the other types of influence, like some sort of political influence or doing me a favor or anything like that, it would not be as effective as just laying out a logical argument about your perspective and why it's the best idea.

This entire paragraph is pure C-style.

BT: How does conflict play out in working with you. How would you define conflict?

Tim: How do I define conflict? So there's varying degrees and when I think of conflict I think of the point where people are on two opposing things that aren't easily resolved. I do a lot of compromise in my work, in my work style, I guess. I try to avoid conflict in general. I do a lot of compromising in order to avoid conflict. If I know that somebody has a perspective and they're really passionate about it, I can take a back seat to that if I don't think it's wrong. When it gets to a point, though, that I've got a way that I think it should be and somebody else has a way that they think it should be, conflict arises.

When it does arise, it becomes frustrating quickly. Though, you know, it'll start off with "here's my point of view" and "here's my point of view" and rather than just working it out and being firm but not being upset about it, I will quickly get to a "Well, if that's the way it's going to be, just forget it then. I'll just do my own thing," kind of approach. As opposed to "No, I think this is the way it should be and that's just it." I get frustrated and don't want to deal with it, and it's all kind of wrapped up in my wanting to avoid conflict. It comes out as frustration. "I don't even want to be talking about this, let's just get it over with" is what my response would appear to be. I think the frustration and impatience is about not wanting to be in conflict at all.

This tension could be the result of a couple of things – Tim's other preferred style might be Steadiness so the tension is between "the right decision" and "avoid conflict." Or his other style preference might be Dominance and conflict is sometimes avoided because it slows everything down.

BT: And so I'd assume at times you're internally conflicted because on one hand you might have a very strong opinion but that strong opinion is in conflict with someone else's strong opinion, so you're kind of now in this stuck area. But if you feel strongly about something, you're not necessarily all that open to compromising?

Tim: Right. Yeah, there's definitely a stubborn streak. I read this great quote, I think it was Margaret Thatcher who said it. It said something like, "I love compromise as long as I get my way in the end." Like that. [laughter] And I think that's kind of the way I operate a lot. Kind of like, "Okay, we'll talk about this and we'll kind of do it this way, but I'm going to have a strategy to flip it in the end." My compromise might be, "Okay, well, we'll see how that works out and then we'll talk about it later." And knowing that this way isn't going to work well, I can then build a case about how it's not going to work well. If I can be patient enough and stubborn enough to then two weeks later say, "Ah-ha! Now we're doing it my way."

BT: It sounds like you are willing to let people go ahead and do something that's not going to work just so they can experience what you already know, that it's not going to work.

Tim: Yes.

BT: Okay. So at times when I'm working with you, in general, I should be a little nervous when you say "Go ahead and do that." Should I challenge you on that, to say "Now, do you believe this is the right way or you're just letting me learn the hard way that it's the wrong way?"

Tim: That would probably be a good strategy. [laughter]

BT: Okay. Next question. What's the best way to compliment you?

Tim: [laughs] There is no good way. Let me think about that, because I'm very uncomfortable with compliments.

BT: Really?

Tim: I'm sort of uncomfortable – I'm happy that they're there, but I'm sort of uncomfortable receiving them.

BT: Why do you think that's the case?

Tim: I don't know. Maybe a shyness thing or not self promotional at all.

BT: So you're not into self-promotion.

Tim: Yeah, but the thing is though, at the same time, that's not really true. I'm just not into outward self-promotion. I don't

feel comfortable saying, "Yep, I did that and it was awesome
and I'm great at it." But I want people to know that I'm
awesome and I'm great at things. So it's not quite there to
say that I'm not into that or it almost gives you the sense
of "Oh, I'm above that. I don't need the praise." I do and I
want it. It's more like indirect praise. For example, knowing
that I worked on something and to say that this thing was
awesome, everybody knows that I worked on this thing and it
even allows me to deflect a little bit by saying, "Oh well, you
know, we all work on stuff and it's great," or "Oh, we're a team
and we all work together," and that kind of thing. Whereas if
somebody said, "Tim
did an awesome job   *Don't be fooled by what appears to be
on this" I would be   humility on the part of a C-style person – a
uncomfortable.   well-delivered compliment about his or her
                         high standards of performance could have a
                         profound impact on the person internally.*

BT: If I said this report
       that was published
       by Tim, Fred, and Shirley is awesome, you would make the
       translation and receive the compliment.

Tim: Yes. Or even if I was the only report author and somebody
        said, "This report is awesome," I could be "Oh, great, well I had
        some people helping me too" and not feel uncomfortable. But
        if somebody said, "Tim, you did an awesome job on this," I'd be
        all squirrelly and say, "Oh, well, thanks, it's nothing."

BT: Now, do you ever have situations where someone compliments
       you, but because of your high standards for yourself, you
       dismiss their compliments because you're thinking, "I could
       have done an even better job."

Tim: Absolutely. But it's more like "Well, I guess it's all right, but
        here's all the problems with it."

BT: What's the best way to give you negative feedback? Let's say
       I'm your manager and I've made some assessment that your
       performance isn't where it needs to be. What's the best way to

give you that feedback?

Tim: Anything is good, it helps me do a better job. I would say feedback in any style other than being insulted. If somebody attacked me as a person rather than my skills, if they said, "You're an idiot," that would not go over well. But if somebody said, "We just did this presentation and I really don't think that you got your message across. I think you could have done that better," that would be great because it's allowing me to then be more perfect.

BT: Is perfection a big deal?

Tim: Yeah. Yeah. I think I definitely want to have everything just right, I want everybody to feel that every product is the best thing that they've seen.

BT: Then, what would be the best way to delegate to you? If I were your manager, what would be the best way to delegate to you?

Tim: I'm constantly volunteering for things but if somebody had a task that they needed me to get done it depends on whether I am working on a bunch of other stuff. I can get tunnel vision on a given task so if somebody tries to introduce something into my tunnel and I'm in that mode, then there'll be a lot of push back from me. "Oh, I couldn't possibly, I've got all these other things." Even if it's some simple little thing that's just going to take five minutes, "Well, you know, I couldn't possibly deal with that now. I've got other stuff to do." Or "it's on my list, I've got it, but, you know, a month from now maybe I can look at this email that you sent me." If I can understand the value and priority of something, I can re-prioritize, if necessary. But my gut reaction is "Oh, I'm not going to deal with it." For example, we're doing this proposal right now and I have a million other things that I'd rather be doing than this proposal, but knowing how important it is that we get more work, I said, "All right. Well, I'll set all this other stuff aside and do this proposal." So...

BT: That's good.

Tim: But I think the better way to set it up if you're giving me something and you know that I'm in tunnel mode would be to market the priority and value of the task. That's the sort of calculation that's going to be going on in my head. "Does this really need to get done?" And I may not be completely balanced in my thinking about that if I'm working on something else. So you should say, "Okay, here's this thing and we really need business and this is going to get us business and I'm certain that we can land this job, and here's the project." In other words, promote the value of it.

BT: How do you tend to handle stress and how would we see you under stress?

Tim: I never tend to feel stress. I'm stressed all the time, but I never, never really feel like there's just too much going on. I'm always dealing with one thing at a time, even though I know there's way too much to handle and big things are happening and things are blowing up. I think when I am stressed, what I do is I get much shorter with my words and how I interact with people. Most of the time I'll sit there and listen to whatever and talk about whatever and just take whatever time and I won't cut people off, unless I'm facilitating the meeting and we need to move things along. But when I'm stressed – keep in mind stress and tons of things to do are synonymous for me – I think that you'd just see a lot of "Well, we don't have time to talk about that now. Let's move on to the next thing. And what are we even here for and why did you do this?"

I have a great example of this when I was working for my former employer. I normally just deal with people screwing stuff up and in this situation we were on this trading floor with all these different people and this guy told me that something was done – it was somebody that I'd known for a while – and it wasn't done right. And it was this big thing, and so I just went off on him in the middle of the floor. "I can't believe that you said this thing was done. When you say something's done it's gotta be done and this is ridiculous. We'll just re-test it all for you." Just started taking the work from him, emasculating him in the middle of the floor. [laughs] That was the far extreme of me being stressed and not being able to take it anymore. I've never been pushed to that point, other than that time, but that would be the extreme of what happens when I'm extremely stressed.

BT: Switching gears a little bit. How do you like to solve problems?

Tim: That's a tough one because I feel like I'm sort of torn between two things. I really like everyone sitting in a room with a white board and throwing ideas out and solving it. But that's not the whole answer because I definitely like internalizing about things. I like having the time to really be able to do that. I think in the perfect world I would be presented with a problem, I would go off, figure out the answer, come back in a room with a bunch of people, and then refine my understanding of that solution. I'd already have a working solution that could then be refined by the group because I wouldn't want to be in the group and not have the answers.

C-style people tend to need to go off and "process" the problem or issue before they feel comfortable in offering solutions – solving problems on-the-fly makes them very uncomfortable.

BT: How do you like to make decisions then?

Tim: Very slowly [laughs]. I definitely do a lot of weighing pros and cons. Right now I'm trying to decide about doing a refinance on my home and there might not be enough value in my property to do a refinance. So I have to decide whether I put some money into the house in order to bring down the loan amount so that the loan to value isn't going to be as high. And I've got a spreadsheet and I've got all these different possible amounts that I could pay. What would the monthly payment be and how much interest is in that, over the two to five years that I would probably have this loan, how much would I save so that I can look at the amount I put in and compare it to the amount that I would get back, and... [laughs] it's just insane. Most people I think would just say "Okay, it didn't make it so I'll either put in money or I won't. Whatever."

BT: How long do you think you spent putting that spreadsheet together?

Tim: I probably spent about an hour and half on it last night. But I had no concept of time while doing it – I just started working on it and then I thought of a new thing to put in there and then a new thing to put in there, and suddenly it's 9:30 and my wife says "it's 9:30." And I say, "Oh, right. You. That's why I'm here." [laughter] Yeah, so I like to make decisions by having all the information that I feel I need to make the decision – endless scenarios and possibilities, facts and figures, a lot of data, a lot of what-if's.

That's why the C-style person can be seen as a procrastinator – endless scenarios and possibilities to consider.

BT: So if you were to pick one of the Microsoft Suite packages – Word, Excel, or PowerPoint – that you would instinctively use to work out a problem or an idea, which one would you go to?

Tim: To answer the question directly, I would say Excel when it's a number problem. If I needed to explain something or figure something out, I would use PowerPoint or Word to be able to draw pictures. But really, if I were trying to solve the problem, I'd go to a white board. It's just easier, I think, to do creative problem solving when you're writing with your hands than trying to draw shapes with an Office product. But to explain that to somebody else, I would use PowerPoint.

BT: Then how do you like to be communicated with?

Tim: I'm not sure if this is exactly what you mean, but if you've got something to communicate to me, put it in an email. I can respond to it on my time. I definitely don't like phone calls. If you've got some list of things for me to look at, or we need to catch up, just put it into an email. Actually I shouldn't say it that way. If you have a list of tasks, just put it into an email. If we need to catch up on something, then we should talk about it, because things come up that wouldn't come up just over email, so it's a more effective way to do status updates and conversations like that.

Very different than the Influence or Steadiness styles.

BT: How irritating would it be if you got a phone call from somebody and the message was, "Tim give me a call when you get a chance. I need to talk to you about some things" and it was a business relationship?

Tim: Not necessarily irritating. But that kind of thing would get answered last. If I have a slew of emails to respond to, and one quick phone call to return, the emails are getting responded to first, and then the phone call is going to happen. And most likely what happens is by the time I get around to the phone call on my list, it's the end of the day and I'm leaving them a message. So if it's something I know I need to follow up with this person … if I know what it is, and I know that it's a priority and I need to call the person, then I'll make time on my list and adjust accordingly. But if it's just the way you described it, "Oh, call me. We need to chat about something," and it isn't dire, urgent, or otherwise, then it's going to the end of the list.

BT: Okay, last question. Best way to get on your good side?

Tim: I think it comes back to just delivering an amazing product. If I'm working with somebody, and the first thing I see out of them is this thing that blows my mind, and it's just like this cool thing that I wouldn't have thought of and is a better product than I would have given direction on or imagined, then that person then becomes infinitely somebody that I trust

and I will go to.
I've never really
seen subsequent
products being
shoddy when
the first one was

Notice how rapport is built for the C-style person by delivering a high quality output rather than establishing an interpersonal relationship like the Influence-style person would aim for.

really good. But I think I would probably give someone leeway if they said, "Okay, well, I know how to work with Tim. I'm just going to really focus on this first thing, and then not pay as much attention to detail in the future because that's not the way I work." I would still have this impression of them that would be hard to break.

PART THREE

Style Combinations
One Explanation for Your Split Personality

Each of us uses at least two of the four styles as our preferred way of doing things, even though we are capable of using all four styles. Regardless of the combination of your two preferred styles, you most likely experience some degree of internal tension as you go about getting things done using your preferred styles. Below are all the possible two-style combinations of the four behavioral styles and a brief explanation of the source of the internal tension and a heads-up on how you may come across to other people.

D-C/C-D Combination

The internal tension is between "get it done now" and "get it done perfectly." So this combination often comes across as "'go go go!' and then 'stop!' – they slam on the brakes and go through the quality checklist, "check, check, check." "Everything perfect?" "Yes." "Then go!" Foot back on the accelerator. No wonder they can have something comparable to a car sickness effect on the people they work with – foot on the accelerator, foot on the brake, back and forth. But where others see speed and quality as an either/or proposition, the D-C/C-D combination finds ways to strike some degree of balance between these unnatural allies. That's how they end up delivering a fairly high quality result in less time than others. They do so by being able to assess risk in real time, in the moment, and make trade-offs that will keep things moving ahead without dangerously compromising quality.

D-I/I-D Combination

The internal tension is between "get it done now" and "is everybody happy?" They want things to go fast, but they also want to make sure everybody is okay with it. So working with them often feels like "go, go, go, go, go!' and then "how's everybody doing? How's the stress level? Is everybody having fun? Yeah? That's great! Now go, go, go, go, go!" You can't blame people for wondering who will show up for work that day, the nice daddy/mommy or the mean daddy/mommy. Sometimes the D-I/I-D person is told they are hard to read, and in some cases "mean." This feedback probably has more to do with people's confusion than reality. For the most part, the D-I/I-D person comes across as easy to work with, very friendly, fun to be with, positive. But then there's this side of them that comes out every so often that is very much the task-master. The stark contrast between the two styles can be quite confusing.

S-C/C-S Combination

Here's what they're thinking. "We have very high standards around here. We expect people to work very hard to achieve these standards. And we know who isn't cutting it because we can't help but size up people and rank order by ability. But we're not going to tell them they're missing the mark because that would be too confrontational and would upset them. Instead, we'll let them figure it out on their own because it must be obvious to them they're not getting the job done, as it is obvious to everyone that works with them." Often when this situation is presented to a S-C/C-S manager this way, they see how unrealistic their expectation is that people will figure out what they are doing wrong on their own. They begin to see the importance of providing feedback to improve performance. But even then the S-C/C-S manager can soften the constructive feedback to the extent that no clear message is sent and none received, resulting in little, if any, performance improvement over time. It's very challenging to find the right balance between maintaining high standards while avoiding conflict.

I-S/S-I Combination

Since this combination is heavily weighted on the "people focus" side, the internal tension is less about "task" versus "people" and more about "team" versus "me." The I-S/S-I person is going to be very focused on the feelings and attitudes of the people he or she works with and will look to create positive, conflict-free work environments to the degree they can. They will invest in the team cohesiveness as the S-C combination does but will more likely want to take a leadership role on the team to ensure things get done in a timely manner and they get some of the spotlight. Whereas the S-C person will be content to work behind the scenes to contribute to the team's cohesiveness and success, a I-S/S-I person will want to be seen and known for their hard work in making the team productive. The internal tension can center around the degree of visibility the I-S/S-I person feels strikes the right balance between being a member of the team who is also an individual. Frustration can set in when the team's progress isn't moving ahead fast enough for their Influence side but they don't feel comfortable in bringing it up to the team, lest they make people uncomfortable and unsure of their capabilities.

Rare Birds

The remaining two combinations are rare because they are direct opposites (as shown on the DISC framework) and therefore share the least in common. But for those individuals who can find the right balance between the opposites, they can end up being highly effective. Here's why.

D-S/S-D Combination

The combination of "drive" with "team orientation" implies that a D-S/S-D person, particularly when in leadership positions, will naturally bring to the situation an ability to influence a group to move forward as a whole. Whereas a high D-style person is usually quite capable and confident of leading the charge, often they find that their followers have lagged behind and need to be re-motivated. Such "circling back" can eat up valuable time, effort, and momentum. On the other hand, even though a high S-style person is usually quite capable and confident of building a cohesive team, often they find that they end up creating such a comfortable environment that the team is not as willing to move ahead with change. But when the two styles are found in one person, there is the potential for the

D-S/S-D person to be able to lead a group through change effectively and efficiently by getting buy-in from the vast majority of the group members. The group may not be the quickest when it comes to implementing change but since buy-in has been secured before the initiative gets underway, there is little disagreement or dissension and therefore time, resources, and momentum are not wasted in "circling back." It is the classic tale of the tortoise and the hare.

I-C/C-I Combination

The combination of "passion" with "perfection" implies that a I-C/C-I person will naturally bring a level of energy and personal identity to reaching their high standards. Whereas a high I-style person is usually quite capable and confident of inspiring and motivating others, often they find that they struggle with defining their aspirations in concrete terms. On the other hand, even though a high C-style person is usually quite capable and confident with setting high standards and mapping out a game plan for personally achieving these expectations, they often struggle with getting buy-in from others to achieve these same expectations. But when the two styles are found in one person, there is the potential for the C-I/I-C person to be able to both inspire and empower others to great heights of achievement. Because of their orientation towards building strong interpersonal relationships, the I-C/C-I person is more likely to emotionally invest in relationships they feel have the potential for exceptional personal growth. Their interpersonal skills play a pivotal role when people's efforts start to fall short of these high expectations. The I-C/C-I person is more likely to verbalize their dissatisfaction with the situation but do so in a motivating, inspirational manner that says "we're capable of so much more than this." Their most tangible contribution to an organization often is, as others have pointed out, they "make creative ideas serve practical purposes."

Practicing the Dialects

Learning to use a particular style dialect takes practice as does learning any other "foreign language." To give people an opportunity to practice speaking the language of a "foreign" style, I created this "style dunking" (versus "language immersion") exercise. Here's how it works:

1. Before the workshop, print off the character descriptions (pages 90-93) on separate sheets of paper, one sheet for each style. It's helpful to use different paper colors to distinguish the four styles. Make enough copies so that every workshop attendee will have his or her own sheet.

2. When you are ready to conduct this exercise during the workshop, share with the class the purpose of this exercise: to help them practice learning and using the language of the behavioral styles through a low-stress role play exercise.

3. You will now need to organize teams of four and try as best you can to have each of the four styles represented in the team, based on their natural style preference. A quick way to do this is to designate each corner of the room as a particular style. Then ask the participants to physically place themselves in whichever corner they feel represents their strongest style preference. This allows you to see how evenly distributed this particular group is when it goes to the four styles.

Warning:

I often use this role-play exercise in my communication skills workshops so it's designed to be used with groups of 12 or more. It also requires that the participants have some background on the four behavioral styles and have either completed a formal or informal assessment that indicates their preferred style(s). You'll find it's a fun exercise that also generates a lot of great discussion about the challenges and benefits of adapting one's communication to their conversation partner.

4. If the distribution is skewed towards some styles more than others, you will need to "recruit" someone whose second highest style preference is the style you need more of and ask him or her to join the style that is under-represented. Just make sure he or she knows they are "representing" that particular style for this exercise.

5. With the four style groups fairly evenly distributed now, simply create teams of four by pulling one person from each of the four style corners and ask the teams to find a spot in the room where they can sit together.

6. Now you will distribute a character description sheet to each team member. You assign the character based on which style is opposite of their natural preferred style. In other words, the person whose top preference is D should be assigned the S character and the person whose top preference is S should be assigned the D character. The same would be true for the people in the team whose top preference is Influence (the C character) and C (the Influence character). What this means is that this exercise is going to force each participant to speak the language of a style that is likely to be unfamiliar (and perhaps even "unnatural") to them.

7. As you distribute the character description sheets, some people will read the heading on the sheet and point out you've given them the wrong sheet. You can tell them that you will explain how this exercise will work in just a moment, once you've finished passing out the character description sheet to each team member.

8. Now you can make explicit that each person has been assigned a character that is most opposite to their natural style to give them an opportunity to hear themselves use the language of that style. Each team member will have a three minute conversation with one other team member, in character. The pairs are grouped by:

    - D character and S character are in one conversation

    - Influence character and C character are in one conversation

9. One pair in the team, one at a time, has a three-minute conversation while the other two people serve as observers.
10. Point out that this is a counter-intuitive exercise in that, the goal is <u>not</u> to have an effective conversation. Rather, the goal is to make sure each person practices using a style most different from their natural style. So each person is to focus on sticking to the style they have been assigned, no matter what their conversation partner says or does. Point out that the observers are there to see where someone "leaks" – where the person's natural style starts to come out. The temptation to do so will be there because the person they will be talking to will be speaking their natural style. But "insist" they resist the temptation and stick to the style they were assigned. Point out that they will probably experience frustration and futility with this conversation as the two of them talk past each other as they stick to their assigned styles. Emphasize this is a good thing.
11. At this point you give them a few minutes to read over their character descriptions. It's helpful to point out that it's usually the D and Influence characters that initiate the conversation once you give the groups the 'go" signal.
12. It's better to synchronize all the teams in the class so that they start the role play on your signal and end it when your timer says 3 minutes is up. To clarify, all of the pairings will have the conversation at the same time (no fish bowl) so it can get fairly noisy in the room, depending on how much fun they are having with this exercise (which they often do). Sometimes you will need to physically spread out the groups of four around the room

to lessen the noise issue.

13. Before giving the first pairing the "go" signal, I often give
everyone a quick character review to help people unfamiliar
with role playing (and still new to the idea of behavioral styles) a
jump start. Here's what I generally say:

- *"For those of you playing the D character, you are all about
moving the discussion forward. No matter what the other
person says to you, no matter what concerns he or she shares
with you, acknowledge their concerns but re-direct them back
to what actions they can going to take to move this project
forward."*

- *"For those of you playing the Influence character, you are all
about making sure the other person is "on board" with this
project – enthusiastic, motivated, and ready to accomplish
great things. If you don't see the enthusiasm, you're going
to be nervous that he or she will not perform at the top of
their ability. No matter what questions they have for you,
keep looking and asking for the enthusiasm you know is so
important to make this project a winner."*

- *"For those of you playing the S character, you will want to
make sure that everything is thought through before diving
in. This project is going to create a lot of change and so a
well thought out plan is needed to ensure things go smoothly.
The more you feel rushed, the more you will want to put the
breaks on because something is going to fall through the
cracks that will have some degree of negative impact on the
project. But you just don't want to tell this person to "slow
down!" Look for ways to get your point across while keeping
everything positive. And don't be surprised if you end up
being a bit stubborn, in a nice way."*

- *"For those of you playing the C character, you will want to
make sure a plan is organized first that reflects the best
research and data so that this is done right the first time.
No matter what is thrown at you, stay focused on getting*

*a detailed plan established with your partner. So far you
haven't seen anything concrete and that makes you very
nervous. Who's going to do what and by when and what data
are we using to tell us this is the right thing to do?"*

14. Give them one last pep talk on having fun with this exercise.
    Encourage them to exaggerate the character, all in the name
    of learning. Once you've confirmed that everyone has finished
    reading their character descriptions and are clear on their
    assignment, get their full attention and give them a "ready, set,
    go" for the first pairing for a three minute conversation.
15. You may need to do some side coaching to keep individuals in
    character and focused on the exercise during the three minutes.
16. Announce when three minutes is up and instruct the observers
    to provide feedback to the role players on where a player stuck
    to his/her assigned style and where there was "leakage."
17. After about 5 to 10 minutes of feedback and team discussion,
    get the class' attention and ask for any great examples of where
    someone demonstrated command of the assigned style and any
    funny examples of where someone's natural style "leaked" into
    the conversation.
18. Now switch so the second pairing has an opportunity to do the
    exercise. Follow the same timing, feedback process, and class
    discussion directions as with the first pairing.
19. Once the second round is finished, with the full class, ask for
    volunteers to share their insights as to what was easier or more
    difficult than they thought it would be in speaking the assigned
    style dialect.
20. To wrap up, ask the class if any of the conversations they
    participated in or observed during the role play exercise
    reminded them of conversations they have had in the "real"
    world – two people talking right past each other. Point out
    that perhaps those conversations were ineffective because both
    persons involved stuck with their preferred style and made
    no effort to adjust to the other's person's style – to speak their
    language.

[Character to be assigned to natural high "S" style participant]

Manager – In-Store Experience (Pizza Pony) ("D" Character)

You are the manager of In-Store Experience for Pizza Pony, a chain of family entertainment centers that features a sit-down pizza restaurant, complemented by arcade games, amusement rides, and live pony rides, all mainly directed at younger children. Your Vice President has asked you to head up a new project that has priority status. Company intelligence has learned that your chief competitor is about to add a 3-D holographic projection to their in-store experience. Your company has been moving in this direction but has had internal squabbles over how much to invest in this.

Your Vice President makes it clear "we" have to move on this fast and she wants you to head this up. You decide to contact the company's manager of digital engineering to get things moving. Clearly your company is behind on this compared to your competition so there's no time to waste. What will probably slow this down is that your digital engineering manager will not have the same sense of urgency as you have in getting this project up and running. He/she comes across as very methodical and ends up slowing everything down. He/she will probably have a lot of questions and remind you of all the details and assignments that will need to be worked out to make an effort like this successful. At this point, you are not interested in figuring out all the details. Rather, you want to make sure he/she is on board in getting going with this project. Now is not the time to slow down. Full steam ahead!

[Character to be assigned to natural high "D" style participant]

Manager – Digital Engineering (Pizza Pony) ("S" Character)

You have just received an e-mail from the Manager of In-Store Experience for the company you both work for, Pizza Pony, a chain of family entertainment centers that features a sit-down pizza restaurant, complemented by arcade games, amusement rides, and live pony rides, all mainly directed at younger children. The e-mail said something about a big project involving getting 3-D holographic projection in the stores ASAP. Doesn't he/she realize the sort of planning that needs to go into an effort like this for it to be successful? This shouldn't surprise you. The manager is known for wanting to take short cuts to get something done. And in other conversations with him/her, you have found yourself doing all that you can to avoid the conversation becoming confrontational. For this conversation, you will want to try to slow down the discussion so that you both can cover all the important details and come up with a plan that will work. But still you are ready for the steamroller. Whatever happened to "plan the work and work the plan?"

[Character to be assigned to natural high "C" style participant]

Manager – In-Store Experience ("I" Character)

You are the Manager of In-Store Experience for Pizza Pony, a chain of family entertainment centers that features a sit-down pizza restaurant, complemented by arcade games, amusement rides, and live pony rides, all mainly directed at younger children. Your Vice President has asked you to head up a new project that has priority status. Company intelligence has learned that your chief competitor is about to add a 3-D holographic projection to their in-store experience. Your company has been moving in this direction but has had internal squabbles over how much to invest in this.

Your Vice President makes it clear "we" have to move on this fast and she wants you to head this up. You decide to contact the company's manager of digital engineering to get some initial ideas started. Clearly your company is behind on this compared to the competition and you want to make sure the Pizza Pony brand doesn't take a big hit. What will probably slow this down is that your digital engineering manager will not have the same enthusiasm for getting this project up and running. He/she comes across as very detail-oriented and ends up slowing everything down. He/she will have a lot of questions and will probably remind you that there are certain procedures in place that need to be followed to make this project successful. He/she often comments on things being too "loosey-goosey" around here. You don't see it that way. You follow established procedures to the point where it makes sense. You would rather leave more room for creativity to blossom. You think, "if we all pull together with the right attitude, we can make this project the best EVER." Let's go team!

[Character to be assigned to natural high "I" style participant]

Manager – Digital Engineering
("C" Character)

You have just received an e-mail from the Manager of In-Store Experience for the company you both work for, Pizza Pony, a chain of family entertainment centers that features a sit-down pizza restaurant, complemented by arcade games, amusement rides, and live pony rides, all mainly directed at younger children. The email said something about a big project involving getting 3-D holographic projection in the stores. The manager mentions a timeframe of "next couple of months." Having worked with this manager before on another project, you anticipate that he/she will want to do things his/her way, and ignore certain standard procedures for developing and executing a project like this. In the process, he/she will end up re-inventing the wheel and that irritates you. You will want to get as many of the details covered during your meeting with the manager. In the past, however, such meetings with him/her haven't gone well. He/she seems to get antsy when you press for details and seems to have another commitment to get to that ends the meeting prematurely. You cringe when you think about his/her usual "positive thinking" mentality. Cut the mumbo jumbo and let's get down to working out the details so we can do things right, the first time.

Acknowledgements

I always assumed authors were simply being magnanimous when they listed name after name in their acknowledgements. The act of putting pen to paper has since enlightened me. For whatever effort I spent alone in putting thoughts and experience into words, this concrete (and hopefully coherent) incarnation of my work was fundamentally (and joyfully) a collaborative effort. Many people generously shared their talents and time with me to make this a better book. If it falls short of its potential, the fault lies entirely with me. My gratitude (and in some cases love) goes to my band of pilgrims. Long may you run.

To Maureen and Dwight, Suzanne, Annette, and Martha, who have been there for me from the beginning, for your heartfelt support. A great deal of what I have accomplished has your finger prints all over it.

To Scott Roubeck, who gives me all the room I need to grow. What a gift.

To Terry Bennett, whose red pen has saved me on more than one occasion. Only you can bring a spirited advocation to the proper use of en and em dashes – who knew?

To Bob Moesta and Chris Spiek, who challenged me to "get it done" faster and better. I won't say I couldn't have done it without you but...

To Tom Crawford, colleague who helped me to see there is a language beyond words, the visual world. Next time I'll have more pictures, promise.

To Aileen Huang-Saad, Jennifer Stovall, Chris Akerley, and Tom Pokorny, for taking the time to sit down with me and reveal your forte and foibles so that others can see what I could only describe. I had so much fun, many, many thanks.

To Regan Borton, who believed in me and this book from the moment we first met. You showed me the way through the maze we call self-publishing.

For all the great people at AuthorHouse and Inscape Publishing who were the consummate professionals I needed them to be in my hours of panic.

www.ingramcontent.com/pod-product-compliance
Lightning Source LLC
Chambersburg PA
CBHW022112170526
45157CB00004B/1600